Jay Ingram

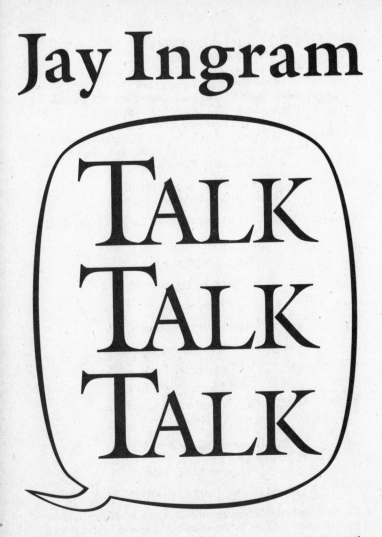

TALK TALK TALK

An investigation into the mystery of speech

Penguin Books

PENGUIN BOOKS
Published by the Penguin Group
Penguin Books Canada Ltd, 10 Alcorn Avenue,
Toronto, Ontario, Canada M4V 3B2
Penguin Books Ltd, 27 Wrights Lane, London W8 5TZ, England
Penguin Books USA Inc., 375 Hudson Street,
New York, New York 10014, U.S.A.
Penguin Books Australia Ltd, Ringwood, Victoria, Australia
Penguin Books (NZ) Ltd, 182-190 Wairau Road,
Auckland 10, New Zealand

Penguin Books Ltd, Registered Offices:
Harmondsworth, Middlesex, England

First published in Viking by Penguin Books Canada Limited, 1992

Published in Penguin Books, 1993

1 3 5 7 9 10 8 6 4 2

Manufactured in Canada

Canadian Cataloguing in Publication Data

Ingram, Jay
Talk, talk, talk

Includes bibliographical references and index.
ISBN 0-14-015611-9

1. Oral communication – Popular works.
2. Speech – Popular works.   3. Psycholinguistics –
Popular works.   I. Title.

P95.I54 1993   401   C92-094127-3

To Rachel and Amelia for teaching me
how children learn language, and to
Cynthia for teaching me about
interrupting.

<<<   # Acknowledgements

I don't even remember what hooked me on language in the first place, but I do know that without the kind of help provided by the people named below, this book would never have got off the ground.

Dr Ian Mackay, a linguist at the University of Ottawa, set me straight on some of the mechanics of Foster Hewitt's "He shoots, he scores," and his colleague Konrad Koerner made clear some of the mysteries of Proto-Indo-European. Neil Smith at the University of London was kind enough to send me some of the research he'd done on Christopher, a linguistic savant. Dr William Samarin made available some of his audio tapes of tongue-speakers, and Dr Myrna Gopnik at McGill took a great deal of time to make sure I had all the information I needed about genes for language. Helen Neville and Julian Jaynes sent me material about their research and answered my questions, as did Geoffrey Beattie at Sheffield University and Susan

Curtiss at UCLA. I am indebted to Aura Kagan at the Aphasia Centre in North York for letting me talk to several people there who put a human face on the condition of aphasia.

Evelyn Chau was in the right place at the right time as far as I was concerned: she did some of the early research that convinced me this book was possible. Writers may sometimes get the feeling that the publisher views their creative output in roughly the same way as a grocer does a shipment of fresh tomatoes (I was once told that my previous book had had "the best cover" of the fall season), but the people at Penguin Canada, especially Cynthia Good, Karen Cossar and my editor, Meg Masters, have succeeded in making me feel at home. And I finally figured out how to sneak page after page past copy editor Mary Adachi without having her obliterate them with notes and questions: just let her cats walk all over the manuscript as you're discussing it.

And of course my family, who are on the front lines of all this, put up with months of my closeting myself on the third floor of our house to finish the book, and I can only promise them that I'll spend more time "at home" now.

Contents

<<< Introduction

This book has come at a perfect time for me, because I've been able to write while listening to my two daughters as they learn to talk. They're typical of most children their age: they don't try very hard, the mistakes they make don't trouble them (if they even notice them) and they are oblivious to the great leaps forward they are making. That is the most striking thing: children learn to express themselves without even realizing that it should be difficult to do. Rachel, when she was five, started to begin the occasional sentence with "Actually ..." Actually?! I know I'd never taught her the meaning of that word—I'm not sure I *could*. And yet the first time she used it, she had it in exactly the right context, even with the reflective pause, head tilted, that should sometimes accompany that word.

Child psychologists have pointed out again and again that children learn both an amazing vocabulary (at a rate of something like ten new words every day) and a set of extremely complicated rules for putting those words into sentences, without anyone explaining how they should do it. Children aren't even told that there *are* rules; they just somehow figure them out—although how is still a puzzle.

It's not just children. We all perform amazing linguistic feats in everyday conversation, and most of the time we'd be completely unable to explain how we knew what to do. The other night I heard this on the radio broadcast of a Toronto Blue Jays game: "Winfield might be even more careful in this at-bat if he were to take the Baltimore–Milwaukee score on the Zurich Insurance Canada out-of-town scoreboard into account." Wow! Winfield would end up leaving his bat on his shoulder if he tried to analyze that sentence! But of course we never waste time analyzing sentences, we just produce them, instantly and without effort, no matter how many clauses, phrases and indirect references they contain.

In fact, complete grammatical sentences are a bit like unspoiled nature: much rarer in reality than in our imaginations. If you could see an exact sound-for-sound transcript of a real conversation, you would be shocked at how incomplete, sloppy and unfinished it is. Half-sentences, parts of words, interruptions: it's almost incomprehensible, at least to the eye. But to the ear? That's different, because even though those words are coming at you faster than theory says you should be able to handle them, you hear them, understand them and can make up an answer instantaneously.

These are just some of the features of language that are still not well understood, and the attraction of all of them is that they are accessible. They're not locked away in the nuclei of atoms, or lost somewhere in remote galaxies. The phenomena that language researchers study are things you can—and do—experience every day, for example, the signals that pass back and forth between partners in conversation to ensure that each gets a turn, or the familiar hesitation of getting caught with a word on the tip of the tongue. You only need to take a minute to look (actually, to listen), and the mysteries of language will make themselves plain to you.

It isn't always fun and games. At the Aphasia Centre in North York, just north of Toronto, adults who have known what it's like to be able to express themselves freely and fluently, sometimes in several languages, are now trying to learn to talk again, and for them the task has none of the delights of childhood. Their language skills have been crippled by strokes, and even those who have taken great strides back towards normal conversation are perfectly aware of how far short they still fall. Talking to them is a startling revelation of how much goes into a typical casual conversation. These people are cut off from a world the rest of us talk our way through with ease.

It's that ease of language that allows us to forget how complex talking is, but if you take a moment to pay attention, you can't help but marvel at it.

Wherever possible in this book, I've tried to show how everyday conversation is full of opportunities for seeing through the superficially simple into the deep, and surprising, world of talk.

1

Lunch with a Friend

You're having lunch with a friend in one of your favourite places to eat, and because you know the menu pretty well and you've actually sat at this very table before, there's nothing novel about the surroundings or the events that unfold around you. This leaves you free to concentrate on the conversation, and you and your friend cover just about all the topics you normally do, from movies and restaurants to politics and relationships. It's the usual sort of conversation the two of you have, and there's little that's really surprising, but think about this: the two of you are able to talk continuously back and forth without ever giving a single thought to *how* you're able to do that. It just seems to happen, but psychologists have barely been able to crack the problem of understanding what goes on between you and your friend as you talk: the social rules you both use to keep the conversation going, and the signals dictated by those rules that you are sending to each other all the time.

Forget for the moment what you're talking about: the choice of topics, and how those topics are introduced and dispensed with; forget too all the other factors that might determine what you're going to discuss, like when you last got together, what's happening to both of you, what's happening in the world or even who's sitting on either side. Just think about the mechanics of your conversation: how it is that you talk for a while, then your friend talks, then you, then your friend. The most elementary aspect of a conversation is how turns are taken, and yet no one today can give you a complete analysis of how this seemingly insignificant process actually works.

Obviously you and your friend *do* take turns, and those turns are beautifully choreographed. Long pauses are awkward, and unless there's a great deal of discomfort or strain in the relationship, very few such gaps will appear in this conversation. Instead you finish speaking, and with hardly time for a breath, your friend starts. Remember, in an hour-long lunch, that's a lot of precision switching back and forth. The puzzle is, how do the two of you pull it off without a hitch?

You both spend much of your time using changes in the sound of your speech, special little code words, and a vast range of non-verbal signals, including everything from gaze and hand movements to changes in sitting position and even foot movements, all telling your conversational partner when it's time to switch.* Psychologists differ on the number of signals and their relative importance, but some are pretty well accepted as being crucial to maintaining an orderly exchange.

First you have to be able to signal when you are finished, or about to finish, your conversational turn. Two American psychologists, Starkey Duncan and Donald Fiske, have identified six different

---

* Some scientists think that hand gestures might represent much more than simple conversational signals. Because talk might have been preceded, aeons ago, by a language of gestures, there is a possibility that hand-waving during talk could still express some of the meaning of what's being said, as well as the rules. One of the most interesting suggestions, by Dr David McNeill at the University of Chicago, is that gestures and talk are assembled and directed by the same processes in the brain, and yet convey different aspects of the whole message. McNeill argues that gestures almost always appear together with speech, and that they often are providing a visual version of what is being said, a sort of 3-D illustration of the words. There are even different kinds of gestures that accompany different sorts of statements. For instance, the sentence, "He keeps trying to catch the snake," could be accompanied by the right hand making a grabbing or twisting motion to suggest the act of trying to catch the snake, *or* the left hand waving slightly to suggest that the action went on and on. (D. McNeill, "So You Think Gestures Are Nonverbal?" *Psychological Review* 92 (1985): 350–371)

ways of letting your listener know that her opportunity is coming.[1] These include a shift in tone, especially changes in the end of a word that we would call a "drawl" (pulling the last syllable out like verbal taffy), the end of some hand movement (a wave or gesture), the interjection of some stock—and meaningless—phrase like "you know," a drop in pitch and/or loudness of voice, or a grammatical cue like the completion of a clause. These psychologists have argued that no one cue is more important than any other, but that the more there are displayed, the stronger the signal to the non-speaker to take over the conversation. It's easy to list them quickly, but these conclusions didn't come easily: it took *two years* to analyze forty minutes of conversation, and the above signals turned out to play the most important role. Duncan and Fiske reported that of 264 smooth exchanges in the conversations they analyzed, 261 were preceded by one or more of these signals.

These signals are of course needed only when it might otherwise be ambiguous as to whether a conversational turn is ending or not. A question, or even a statement like "I hear you went to the reunion ..." indicates you want a response. But most of the time the situation isn't that clear, and that's when these signals come into play.

But sending the signal to change speakers isn't the end of the story. The listener has to respond by starting to talk, and as soon as that happens, the original speaker has to stop. If that three-step sequence is followed, then the conversation will switch repeatedly and smoothly back and forth. But the speaker can complicate matters by sending two messages at the same time: one a signal to switch, like a change in tone, and the second, a gesture, like a fist, meaning "Do not take over this conversation." This somewhat threatening gesture, which researchers call a "tense" hand position, apparently works, because listeners rarely ignore its message not to talk.

Meanwhile the listener is not passive. He (or she—there actually may be a significant difference, as we will see) may interject words or sounds, using what's been called the "back channel." These are responses like "uh huh," "yeah," "m-hm" that come right in the middle of the partner's turn. But they don't come in on top of words— back-channel talk is usually timed to fall into slight pauses left by the speaker, and in fact it is solicited too, either verbally, by the completion of a clause or sentence, or by your friend turning his gaze towards you. Whether your back-channel interjection falls into a space or not, it is followed by your friend shifting his gaze away from you, letting you know that he is about to continue. What's fascinating is that these little back-channel mutterings (or even nods and smiles) are not inhibited by the closed fist signal, suggesting that they are not interpreted by the speaker as attempts to seize the floor. They're really reinforcement, encouragement that he is being listened to, and they're also a clear indication that the partners in a conversation are both listeners and talkers at the same time. If one partner doesn't give back-channel signals, like the reassuring "uh huh" or even just a nod of the head, the conversation will grind to a halt.

Back-channel signs send no message that you want to take over—there are more appropriate ways to do that, by an obvious shift in body position, or a sudden and noticeable intake of breath. And some partners in conversation (although probably not a friend) may stave off such attempts to take over by introducing his turn with an expression like "First of all ..." (uh oh, this is really going to be long), or interrupting the flow in the middle by saying, " ... and that's not all ..." (is there really more?), then " ... and finally ..." If he senses you still want to converse, he may use the imperious gesture of holding his hand up, palm facing you, that tells you not to interrupt.*

The precision of all this is striking, even when it appears not to be. This constant changing back and forth from speaker to listener is usually clean and rapid, producing a conversation in which only one person is talking at any time. But not always: sometimes the listener begins to speak a little too soon, and overlaps the end of the other person's final few words. But this apparent sloppiness, or

---

* I've probably done thousands of radio interviews, and the ones that strike fear into the heart most are those in which the interviewee begins by saying, "There are four good reasons for saying this ..." A close second are those which begin, "Let me give you some of the background to this ..."

impatience, has been viewed as evidence for even greater conversational accuracy than you might have imagined.

In a report in the language journal *Semiotica* in the early 1970s, Gail Jefferson argued that what appears in this case to be a simple interruption is actually another device for keeping conversation orderly.[2] In many of these instances the listener adds words that would make a sensible finish to the sentence, or actually finishes the sentence with exactly the same words as the speaker is saying. The reasons for this can vary: sometimes the listener is indicating that he already knows what the speaker is about to say, and by overriding her is in effect saying, "I know what you're about to say, and I already know that." If he waited until the end of the statement, the claim of foreknowledge wouldn't carry as much weight. There is what I'd call the "Reach for the Top" risk though: just as the overzealous contestant hits his buzzer too soon and ends up answering the wrong question, so too could the conversationalist finish the wrong sentence—that's the price you pay for wanting to appear knowledgeable.

What's amazing is that the timing can be so incredibly accurate that the two people can be saying the same words at the same time. In some cases, admittedly, it's easier than I'm making it sound: most conversations end with an agreed-upon package of expressions like "See you," "Talk to you soon," "Okay," and "Bye" that make it easy to overlap. But that doesn't take away from those interjections which come in the middle.

It's accepted by analysts that we all send signals to move a conversation along. The question is, which of these are the most important and why? It might be that Drs Duncan and Fiske had the right idea about signals, but weren't right that any one signal is as important as the next. Some of the most interesting recent research has been to try to rank the status of these signals.

English researchers Ann Cutler and Mark Pearson have tested the idea that the pitch of a person's voice at the end of his turn changes and alerts his partner to take over.[3] In particular, they wanted to find out if drops in pitch on words in the middle—which aren't intended to signal a switch—could be reliably distinguished from drops in pitch at the end. They had speakers read dialogues that contained exactly the same phrases appearing at different places. The first version in one example was:

"Foster was pretty upset you rejected his design—any particular reason?"

"It's simply not good enough and *that's all I have to say on the subject!* I don't see why I have to justify my decisions."

"Okay. Sorry I asked."

The second version switched the position of the key sentences:

"I don't see why I have to justify my decision. It's simply not good enough, and *that's all I have to say on the subject!*"

There were several exchanges like this, some in

which the participants were agreeing, some like the one above, where they weren't. The tapes were cut so that the same phrases, which had originally appeared either in the middle or at the end of statements, were given to judges to see if they could tell which was which. The judges did succeed in distinguishing final phrases (those that would cue the listener to take over the conversation) from middle phrases, but they weren't consistently good at it. Some of the speakers gave them a lot of trouble, and in fact they were only able to tell which was which with good accuracy when the tape was taken from conversations in which there was disagreement. This led to the fascinating conclusion that in an argument you probably take extra care to apply the right pitch (going up rather than down) on words that are ending a sentence or a clause because you are anxiously trying to stave off interruption! (Incidentally the judges failed completely to distinguish ends from middles using a typed transcript, suggesting that the actual words and their meanings have nothing to do with triggering changes in speakers.)

A colleague of Ann Cutler's, Geoffrey Beattie of Sheffield University, has done his own investigation of the importance of gaze on speaker-switching in conversations.[4] Gaze plays a key role in conversation: you always look into the other person's eyes more when you're listening than talking, and you tend to look away when you're composing the next few sentences in your head, only to meet the other's eyes again when you're already in full conversational flight. (If you don't look away when you're planning what you're going to say, you're much more likely to commit speech errors, especially false starts.) Listeners too gaze raptly at the speaker: if they don't they will be perceived as not being interested in what's being said. But most important, gaze has always been assumed to be a trigger for change: if the speaker finishes talking and looks directly into the eyes of the listener, it's time to change. If, on the other hand, she shifts her gaze, she's saying she wants to continue.

There are differences between the sexes too, the biggest being that women in conversation spend much more time looking at each other ("mutual" gaze) than do men: thirty-eight percent versus twenty-three percent. Even so, the length of each episode of eye contact between women is very brief, averaging something like a second and a half. Incidentally, gazing at someone does *not* mean you are staring straight into that person's eyes. Usually your eyes wander all over, sometimes tracing a line down the nose, or flitting across an eyebrow, or moving restlessly back and forth across the lips. That's when you're sitting at some sort of normal distance. I realized years ago that when I was doing radio interviews, even though I didn't dare take my eyes off the interviewee, for fear of looking bored, I *never* looked anyone in the eyes—always at the mouth. This was especially true if I were sitting close enough to be able to hold a microphone to the person's mouth. No one ever mentioned that they thought this was odd behaviour on my part!

Geoffrey Beattie tested the importance of gaze in the simplest way imaginable: by analyzing telephone conversations. If gaze plays a central controlling role in how you pass the conversational baton to your partner, then talking on the telephone should be more cumbersome, unless some other signalling mechanism takes over. Beattie and his colleague Phil Barnard collected tapes of seven hundred calls to directory assistance over a four-month period. After looking at the transcripts of these calls, they chose eighteen for detailed study, ranging in length from twenty-eight to four hundred and ninety-two words. After eliminating the pauses that are associated with questions and answers, or with the operator having to look up a number, Beattie compared the length of pauses that occurred during a switch in speakers on the telephone, with the same sorts of pauses in a face-to-face conversation, and found that there was no difference! In addition, two telephone speakers start to talk at the same time no more often than two people do when they are face to face, and they actually interrupt less! It seemed from this experiment that not having access to the gaze of your conversational partner created absolutely no barrier to switching speakers successfully and smoothly. But how can this be—is there some other cue that we use when we're on the phone?

It appears that the people in this study compensated with what's called a "filled pause" (an "ah," "um" or "er") stuck in where normally, in a face-to-face situation, there would be only a silent pause. Uttering a filled pause before you actually say any words is a way of letting the other person know that you are indeed about to begin your turn, and in this case speakers used them four times as much as they probably would have had they been looking at each other. On the telephone, an "unnhhh" secures the speaker's role for you, especially important in a formalized exchange with a directory assistance operator, a situation which the experimenters admit is not a typical one. This study shows that while gaze may be important in face-to-face (or heart-to-heart) talks, it is not essential to grease the wheels of conversation. And why should it be, when you consider that humans have always been able to talk to each other in the dark, and it's probably true that early cave conversations were replete with "filled pauses."

The picture I've painted of your lunch conversation is idealized: a dialogue in which turns are taken smoothly and discretely, as you and your friend operate according to a mutually understood set of signals and rules. Of course any two friends will have developed their own style, and may use all the signals mentioned above and many others, or may have dispensed with some of the common signals as unnecessary for talking with someone who is familiar. The whole effort moves very fast, and is complicated by many factors that these analyses can't even take into account—they are merely the skeleton on which the clothes of actual day-to-day conversations are draped. So signals shouldn't be misinterpreted as being the whole story, but they do play an important and probably fundamental role in guiding conversation. And what happens when the rules break down, and turn-taking gets disrupted? Interruptions. That is next.

2

<<< Don't Let Me Interrupt
You

I was telling a linguist that I was going to write
about how the smooth exchanges of conversations
can be disrupted, and she said, "You're going to
talk about how men interrupt women all the
time?" Well, I told her I was, but it turns out that
the evidence for the male domination of conversation isn't quite as overwhelming as I expected,
given that so many people seem to have heard it
and believe it to be true.

The theorists who have identified the signals
which ensure smooth conversation realized there
could be breakdowns in this system. A blatant
example would be if one partner just didn't bother
responding to anything the other said. Breakdown
could also result if one person spoke out of turn: if
he interrupted. Both of these potential hazards to
conversation were highlighted by research done by
American sociologists in the late 1970s, and their
research helped solidify a suspicion that, in con-

14

versation as in life, men attempt to dominate women.

Dr Pamela Fishman was one of these investigators[5]: she taped fifty-two hours of conversations from three couples at home in their apartments; all of them were between twenty-five and thirty-five, and all professed to be sympathetic to the women's movement.* She soon found that there were clear indicators that the women had to work harder in these conversations than the men, and the words they used, and the way they phrased their talk reflected this. A perfect example was the introduction of a new topic of conversation. In Fishman's tapes, men introduced twenty-nine new topics, and twenty-eight of those actually turned into conversations. Women, on the other hand, tried out forty-seven topics of their own, of which only seventeen were raised to conversational status. Fishman argued that there was no significant difference in content between the men's and

---

* Even so, from the beginning there were signs of asymmetries in the responsibilities or rights within each couple. Turning the tape recorders on and off was left to each couple's discretion, and Dr Fishman reported that in each of the three, the men always turned the tape recorders on and off, and sometimes they even did it without the wife's knowledge. ("It's okay, honey, I'll handle the technology"—my quote, not hers.) One of the men even took the trouble to erase the time-cueing clicks on the tape, saying he wanted the tape to sound smoother. Hmmmmmm.

women's topics (they were all about friends, something in the paper or an event that day), and that what determined whether or not a new topic actually stimulated some sort of exchange was the reaction of the person responding to it. In this study the men nipped a lot of conversational topics in the bud by their lack of response, and although Dr Fishman isn't explicit about how they did it, you can imagine that a "Hmmhh," or a "Yeah, really?" would probably do the job. Complete silence would be pretty effective too. On the other hand, women responded somewhat more enthusiastically to men's topics, with the result that those became the topics of conversation. (Of course, these *were* couples, with their courting days safely behind them. One can only imagine how much more eagerly these men would have grasped at any conversational straws in their bad old bachelor days.)

What was more interesting in this study were the signs in women's speech that they were aware that their conversational gambits were failing (and perhaps in these relationships always failed at roughly the same rate) and were trying to fan the flames. One common trick was for a woman to use a question at the beginning of what she was saying. Women's topics introduced by a question became subjects of conversation thirteen times out of eighteen (compare that with the overall rate of seventeen out of forty-seven). As many as a third of these questions could easily have been rephrased as statements, the only thing making them questions being the addition of some little phrase like "Isn't it?" or "Couldn't we?" This suggested they were being used to guarantee a response: after all, a statement, strictly speaking, requires nothing from the listener, but a question demands at least an answer.

Pamela Fishman found other telltale signs that the women in this study had noticed the flagging conversational interest of their mates, and were trying to arouse it. Beginning with phrases like "This is interesting" or "You know" is an attempt to gain the attention of the listener—they are little phrases that are in essence admissions that whatever follows may not be interesting enough in and of itself to be worthy of attention. In Fishman's study, women used questions two and a half times as often as men, phrases like "this is interesting" twice as much, and "you know" five times as much.*

Other research has identified pauses as a sign of trouble too: if they come at the end of what you've just said, you immediately suspect that your partner feels there's nothing worth responding to, and the lack of confidence that results leads some to start dropping pauses into the middle of sentences, hoping against hope for some sort of comment.

At about the same time that Pamela Fishman's apartment tapes established the conversational importance of response, or more important, the

---

* For more on "You know," see Chapter Nineteen.

lack of it, Candace West and Don Zimmerman were investigating the other end of the spectrum: interruptions.[6] They taped casual conversations between good friends in settings like a coffee shop, a drug store and other public places, and found that in conversations between men and women, the men were responsible for an amazing forty-six of a total of forty-eight interruptions! (And this doesn't include some instances of talking at the same time.) In Chapter One, I mentioned that some examples of talking at the same time can be interpreted as reinforcing or exclaiming: these are usually brief and don't necessarily disrupt the speaker's turn. In this study, by contrast, only "deep" interruptions were counted, these being interruptions that started more than two syllables before the end of a speaker's turn, and appeared to disrupt what that person was saying. (Some interruptions don't require one person to talk over another at all—they can just jump in when the speaker, although pausing briefly, has every intention of continuing.) One other interesting note was that the males interrupted females on average at a point when they were twelve syllables into their turns, while females waited twice as long—twenty-five syllables—before interrupting.

The overwhelming preponderance of male-initiated interruptions in this study drew comparisons to parent-child conversations in which the parents are supposed to do all the interrupting. (As a parent I *really* want to see that data.) I'm sure that this was the study my linguist friend had in the back of her mind when she checked to make sure I was including the evidence that "men interrupt women all the time." Yet not all researchers have acclaimed this study: critics have pointed out that of the 46 interruptions, 11 were contributed by one man (I know—you had lunch with him just the other day), leaving an average of only 3.5 for the other ten men in the study. That was another point: the sample was very small, and therefore potentially unrepresentative. And maybe the most important criticism was that in many cases, interruptions may not represent acts of aggression. We've all been involved in hilarious, high-energy conversations in which everyone is talking at the same time, and nobody is offended. The context is the salt grain with which studies like this must be taken.

To their credit, West and Zimmerman were cautious about their results, believing that using people who already knew each other well may have given a biased impression of how much men would interrupt women. So they did a similar study, this time in a laboratory situation in which they monitored the conversation between men and women who had just met. And indeed the striking disparity in interruptions did not reappear, although the effect was certainly still there. This time twenty-one out of twenty-eight interruptions were by males. (Well, it doesn't seem that much compared to forty-six out of forty-eight.) This second study also added some insight into what people do when they are interrupted. In general there are a number of possibilities, ranging from the feisty (just keep talking, louder and louder if necessary, until the interrupter backs off) to the abject (stop talking *and* encourage the interrupter by asking about what he just said). Between these extremes lies a series of responses, all of which amount to surrender: stop talking immediately but don't encourage the intruder, keep talking until you're finished a complete thought and then pick up what was said in the interruption, or (tougher yet) persist until you finish your thought, then stop talking. Of course this doesn't cover the entire range of possible responses—some people recycle a phrase over and over until the interrupter stops talking, at which point the phrase is suddenly heard, and the person regains the floor—but it illustrates what's possible.

Despite the fact that these studies showed that men interrupt more than women, it was a surprise to see that men and women respond in the same way to being interrupted. With rare exceptions, neither sex fights an interruption, preferring instead to use one of the above strategies to back out of the clash.

It's still unclear how Zimmerman and West's studies apply to everyday social situations, although remember they found more interruptions by men in what you would think were "natural" settings. Linguist Deborah Tannen, author of *You Just Don't Understand*, makes the point that you can't just apply these principles willy-nilly, without taking into consideration the conversational styles of the people involved, how well they know each other, and what they're talking about: what might be an interruption to you mightn't be to me, or an interruption by a friend might not be as offensive as one by a colleague. She sees conversation between men and women not so much as a power struggle but as a clash between styles: men using talk to establish their status, women to create intimacy. (Which might explain why the men in Pamela Fishman's couples were so uninterested in having conversations with their women—they'd already established their status, so why talk?) Other experimenters have shown that in situations with more than two people, women interrupt just as much as men do, but again these are studies of university seminars, and it's been suggested that in situations like that, where it's important to make an impression, interruption could be one of the tools for doing that. Such experiments might therefore be saying nothing more about the kinds of situations we all find ourselves in than either the casual chats or the lab conversations studied by Zimmerman and West.

Much of the research on interruption in the 1970s was undertaken to dispel the idea that women were interrupted more because they allowed it to happen—that they had some sort of defensive conversational posture which invited interruption. However widespread that idea had been, sociologists correctly interpreted it as part of a continuum of thinking that taken to its extreme justified actual violence to women. While there was no evidence uncovered in these studies of any sort of conversational style that would invite interruption, the question remained, why *are* women interrupted more, at least in one-on-one chat?

It is commonly believed (apparently) that women talk more than men. If this belief is widely held, then perhaps men interrupt more to "get a word in edgewise." Ann Cutler of the Medical Research Council in England set up the following experiment to find out if both sexes perceive women to talk more than men.[7] She and her colleague Donia Scott selected four excerpts from plays, each of which involved two speakers. Here's an example of part of one of the dialogues:

"Now then ..."

"Now then what?"

(contemptuously) "Now then what!"

"I don't know what you're talking about."

"Oh you don't, don't you?"

"No I don't, so shut up."

Scott and Cutler then had these short conversations recorded by actors in the following combinations: both parts read by females, both by males, and two versions of male and female, each sex taking a turn being the first speaker. The duration of each speaker's part was timed to the nearest hundredth of a second, and then the tapes were played to judges who had to estimate who spoke more in each conversation.

In those tapes where the roles were played by two women or two men, judges estimated the time each took to be almost exactly the same. But when the roles were played by a man and a woman, the women were judged to be talking more, regardless of who took the role of the first speaker—even though in every case exactly the same words were being read! And it didn't matter who was doing the judging: women perceived women to be talking more too.

Cutler and Scott were unable to identify exactly why this happens. They were working with two theories in mind: one was that because women's voices are higher-pitched than men's, and most of us talk in a higher-pitched voice if we are talking faster, the woman's voice might seem as if it's producing words faster, and so talking a lot. Another possibility is that because the importance of women's contributions to society have traditionally been undervalued, there is a perception that what they have to say can't be important, and so *any* amount of time taken up by a woman speaking is, by definition, a long time. Cutler and Scott succeeded in proving that both men and women *do* overestimate the amount women talk, but they cannot be sure which of the two explanations is correct—they suspect it might be some of both. There could, of course, be other explanations for this misperception of how much women talk: Pamela Fishman's research showing that women were constantly trying to establish topics of conversation suggests that these women might be seen to be talking all the time, in their desperate attempts to get some kind of response.

The last word on interruptions goes to the same

Geoffrey Beattie who did the study of turn-taking in telephone conversations mentioned in Chapter One.[8] In the late 1970s, when Margaret Thatcher was still an opposition politician in Great Britain, Beattie taped and analyzed a television interview with Thatcher, and compared it with a separate television interview with the then Prime Minister, James Callaghan. In the beginning Beattie was looking at the process of taking turns (you'd think a very artificial exchange in an interview of any kind), but found that the interruptions told a fascinating tale.

More than a third of all switches from one speaker to the other were by way of interruptions, which perhaps doesn't come as much of a surprise, given the sometimes combative nature of political interviews, coupled with the time constraints of television. But the surprise was that Margaret Thatcher—the Iron Lady—was interrupted or overlapped twice as much by her interviewer as she interrupted him. In the other interview, the roles were almost exactly reversed: the relaxed and friendly James Callaghan did the majority of the interrupting. In particular, Thatcher's interviewer, Dennis Tuohy, butted right in eleven times, while Thatcher didn't butt in on him once!

When Geoffrey Beattie examined the videotapes of the interview, it appeared that there was something going on beyond the usual interviewer aggressiveness. For one thing, Thatcher did live up to her tough image by persisting in the face of interruptions much longer than most people would. Sometimes she continued to talk for five seconds after the interruption, where in normal circumstances half a second is more typical. But why was she being interrupted so often? Was this another example of male dominance? Geoffrey Beattie thinks not. He theorized that Margaret Thatcher was being interrupted because she was sending out the signals that would normally mean she was about to yield her turn—the only problem being that Thatcher wasn't ready to yield, and when Dennis Tuohy read the signals and started to talk, he interrupted her.

In this interview Thatcher was often interrupted shortly after she had come to the end of a clause, dropped the pitch of her voice, and drawled one of the last syllables: all three have been listed as signals to switch, and three together would normally be considered a virtual order to take over. Here's one such moment:

Thatcher: "The police do a fantastic job—"

Tuohy: "Coming—"

Thatcher: "—and we must support them in every way possible."

Tuohy: "Coming toward the end of our time ..."

Apparently Thatcher drawled the last syllable of "fantastic," and also dropped the pitch of "job," which in turn marked the apparent completion of that thought. Nor did she signal Tuohy *not* to take over, by a gesture, or even by a filled pause, an "ummm" or something like that. Beattie tested this idea by taking short extracts from various places in the interview, including Thatcher in the middle of a statement, at the end when there was no interruption, and also where there were interruptions. Judges had to guess whether or not Thatcher had come to the end of what she was saying, and the verdict was clear: in those places where she had been interrupted, she sounded to the judges as if she had finished; in places where she was about to go on without interruption, they agreed she seemed about to continue.*

Beattie was even able to conclude that the problem lay in the cues Thatcher gave the interviewer. They were hybrids—halfway between ending and not ending. The pitch of her voice fell quickly, as it does at the end, but not very far, as is the case when she intends to continue. When she had completed what she wanted to say, she always gazed straight at Dennis Tuohy. When she was going on to something else, she only looked at him about half the time. Again, just prior to an interruption, it was ambiguous: she was looking at him about eighty percent of the time. Beattie wondered if the

---

* Of course in experiments like this nothing is ever one hundred percent. There was a statistically significant tendency for the judges to hear Thatcher's comments before an interruption to sound finished, but it wasn't unanimous. Nor has the reception given this experiment been unanimous. I'll spare you the details, but to date there has been a published critique, then a response to that critique by Beattie, then a reply to Beattie's response, then a final (we hope) rejoinder to the reply. And that's where it stands today.

speech training Thatcher had received (to equip her with an accent more appropriate to British public life than she already had) had interfered with her normal signalling, creating these interruptive moments.

The frustrating thing about these experiments is that they each illuminate only one tiny facet of conversation, and it would be a mistake to take any of them to be the gospel truth—the situations in which we find ourselves talking to others are just too varied for us to be doctrinaire about what's happening. On the other hand, once you've learned about the signals we all use for taking turns, I guarantee you conversation will never be the same again. You'll find yourself listening for back channels, waiting for gestures, and categorizing your own response to being interrupted. At least it'll get you through the dull ones.

3

<<<

It's How You Say It

On March 22, 1923, a Canadian legend first cried out the words that were to make him famous; words that now qualify as the best-known Canadian phrase: "He shoots, he scores!" On that night Foster Hewitt broadcast a hockey game between Toronto Parkdale and Kitchener from the Mutual Street Arena in Toronto. At some point in the evening, he said, "He shoots, he scores!" but as Foster admitted later, he didn't really remember exactly when, because he had no idea the phrase would become as famous as it did.

It is a short, simple phrase, and Foster must have shouted it tens of thousands of times during his long career. Simple, and yet not so simple. It's only four words, but producing even those four demands a complexity, precision and speed of movement that could hardly be followed if you were watching in slow motion. Millions of Canadians know the phrase and could name the man who made it famous, even though it probably sounded slightly different every time he said it. But few of those have any idea what it takes to say it. Before you can appreciate the anatomy, physiology and neurology of what happened when Foster Hewitt said, "He shoots, he scores!" you need a run-down on the equipment which was involved: air from the lungs, a voice-box, the soft palate, tongue, lips, teeth, ears and brain.

Starting from the bottom, the lungs: normally we breathe in and out fifteen times a minute—one full breath every four seconds—just to move enough oxygen around our bodies to keep us alive. But the normal situation is rare for humans. Even though speaking evolved much more recently than breathing, it's had a profound impact on how we breathe. When we speak, the rate and timing of breathing follows the patterns of speech: pauses for breath come at the ends of sentences, clauses and paragraphs. It's also been claimed that the amount of air you take in is about the amount you'll need to be able to say what your brain has already planned (and that can vary from half a second to forty seconds' worth). And if you suddenly and unpredictably need to search for a word, you'll hold your breath while you do it, because otherwise you would disrupt the careful—but unconscious—rationing of air for the words you've planned to utter. I say "claimed" because it seems to me that in most conversations we don't plan our next few sentences all that carefully, and so we're often either left with plenty of air in our lungs and nothing else to say, or gasping out the last few words of what turned out to be (literally) much more long-winded than we'd hoped.

Inhaling for talking is much faster than normal inhalation. But exhalation is much slower, so that more words can be spoken as the air flows out. The result is that when you talk you spend much more of your time breathing out than breathing in: about ninety-five percent versus five percent. This isn't as simple as it sounds, because the air pressure in your lungs is higher just after you've inhaled—so you unconsciously regulate the flow of air with your diaphragm and the muscles in your ribs, gradually switching from the set used for inhalation to those specialized for exhalation. You can, of course, talk while you're inhaling, but most of the time when you're doing that you're actually producing a loud whisper, not ordinary speech.

Somehow that air has to be able to create sounds on its way out, and that's where the voice-box comes in. Larynx, Adam's apple, voice-box— it's all the same. It feels hard in your throat because the main piece of cartilage that forms the outer shell of the larynx is in front. There are other pieces of cartilage, and an elaborate set of muscles. All the air that comes up from your lungs flows through the larynx, and in doing so passes between two muscles on the inside that stretch across the airway. Each has a whitish ligament running along the edge—those are the vocal cords. Obviously they're not actually *cords*, but the French scientist Ferrein gave them that name in

1741 because he thought they produced sound like the strings of a violin. They don't, and scientists now call them the vocal *folds*.

When you're just sitting breathing quietly, there is a roughly triangular space between the two vocal cords through which air passes. But the muscles in and around the larynx can pull together the small pieces of cartilage attached to the back ends of the vocal cords, and close the space between them. This is actually what you do if you stand up from a sitting position, or lift a heavy object. You close the vocal cords completely, trapping air in your chest and giving your chest muscles something to brace against. But helping you get out of a chair is a minor diversion for your larynx: by far its most important role is to direct food and drink to the stomach, bypassing the lungs. Failure to do that could be fatal. In humans, the vocal cords in the larynx have come to serve as the fundamental machinery for speech.

As you're reading this, your vocal cords are probably apart, with air flowing past them, in and out, every four seconds. Put your fingers on your voice-box, and suddenly make the cartoon noise for sleeping: Z-Z-Z-Z-Z-Z-Z-Z-Z. You'll be able to feel it with your fingers as well as hear it. The instant you decided to make that noise, signals from your brain arrived at the muscles controlling the vocal cords, commanding them to close. They closed until they were almost touching, forcing the air that had been passing quietly through the open space between them through a much narrower opening. The result is similar to pursing your lips and blowing. Your lips vibrate rapidly, allowing a tiny puff of air out each time they're open, and you make the sound that horses in western movies always make when they're reined in at the hitching post. If you purse your lips a little tighter, you get the sound called the "raspberry."

The vocal cords vibrate and emit puffs of air at a very rapid rate: the average time between puffs for men is something like eight-thousandths of a second, giving time for 120 puffs *every second!* That produces a tone that is a little more than an octave below middle C on the piano. Women's vocal cords are on average usually shorter, so they vibrate faster and are higher pitched. The average for women is 220 puffs per second: two black keys and a white below middle C. That's a puff every four and a half thousandths of a second.

But that's only an average. The musculature of the larynx is so complicated that you can control the tension in the vocal cords, their length (by changing the angles that different pieces of cartilage make with each other), their shape, and whether they're in contact over their entire length or parted slightly, like a shirt forced open at the bottom by a beer belly. To give you an idea of how precisely you can control your vocal cords, first whisper (during which your vocal cords are slightly open and not vibrating at all), then change to a "stage" whisper. Suddenly your vocal cords have moved from a position in which they're near each other but not touching, to being closed shut for much of their length, but open at one end.

Changes like this will change the pitch of the sound coming from the larynx—maybe by as much as a couple of octaves—and we use those differences in pitch to communicate differences in meaning. A falling pitch at the end of a word like "no" or "yes" usually indicates a definite statement; a rising pitch suggests doubt or questioning. Tone of voice, which communicates so much more than just the words of conversation, is dictated largely by changes in the vocal cords.

But even though the vocal cords are capable of producing a wide range of sounds, and altering those sounds by sliding them up and down in pitch according to the intent of the message, this still leaves you far short of actual talk. You have to add the specific sounds of consonants and vowels, and this is where lips, tongue, soft palate (the roof of your mouth at the back) and teeth come in.

Every speech sound starts with the air coming up from the lungs, whether it's flowing smoothly or being puffed through the vocal cords. Vowels like **ah**, **oo** and **ee** are made by changing the shape of the space in which those sounds can reverberate. That includes the whole airway from the top of your voice-box, up the back of your throat, over your tongue, past your teeth and between your lips. You can also move that air through your nostrils by dropping the soft palate (the back half of the roof of your mouth, from which dangles the funny little tear-drop-shaped uvula).

You can make this airspace longer by pouting,

or shorter by pulling the corners of your mouth back, as in smiling. You can open your mouth, or close it down. From a sound engineer's point of view, all of these actions are just changing the shape and length of the tube the sound is travelling through, and that alters the quality of the sound.

Each vowel has, among the variety of different tones within it, some pitches or frequencies that are more prominent than others, and these are unique to every voice. In 1991 a computer program called SpeechStation, which can tease these frequencies out of recorded speech, proved that the recordings of some of Winston Churchill's most famous wartime speeches were actually made by an actor! When Churchill made those speeches during the war, recording was not allowed inside the House of Commons. He usually made the speeches, then recorded them later, complete with echo effect to simulate the Commons. But he was sometimes too busy for the recording, and he authorized the use of a stand-in, an actor named Norman Shelley. But until this recent analysis, it wasn't clear how many (if any) of the existing recordings purporting to be Churchill were really Shelley. (There were claims that eventually Churchill had recorded them all, even the ones first done by the actor.)

A company in Massachusetts called Sensi-metrics used the computer program to trace the predominant vowel frequencies in fifteen of the Churchillian speeches recorded in a studio.

Twelve had Churchill's speech patterns—they were identical to those found in recordings of public speeches where it's certain that Churchill was indeed the speaker—but three were obviously the voice of someone else, presumably Norman Shelley. And what a trio of speeches: the first was when Churchill/Shelley promised Britain "blood, toil, tears and sweat"; the second contained the famous phrase, "their finest hour," and the third, "We shall fight them on the beaches, in the fields, in the streets and in the hills." As perceptive as we are of slight sound differences in the speech of others, it took a computer program to reveal when Churchill's vowels weren't really Churchill's vowels.

Consonants are completely different. If vowels are differences in sound that we create by squeezing and moulding the space through which air is flowing, consonants *interrupt* that flow and add noise to it. Some consonant sounds are little explosions created when air builds up behind sealed lips, then is suddenly released. Sometimes narrow openings are created which force air to hiss its way through. The tongue can even stuff itself in the airway, blocking it completely.

Let's go back now to the gondola in Maple Leaf Gardens, on any wintry Saturday night from the thirties through the seventies. Once, twice or even three times through the evening, you might hear, "He shoots, he scores!" Here is what was really going on as Foster Hewitt gave voice to those words:

In the first split second, his vocal cords open and air is forced through them, but they aren't yet vibrating (the **h** in "He ..."). At the same time, the lips spread, and the tongue moves quickly forward and up, cutting off most of the oral cavity behind it and creating a separate (but tiny) air space between it and the teeth. Almost before the tongue is in place, the lips begin to move again, this time closing down into a rounded shape from their original spread position. By now the vocal cords are buzzing, but the **ee** sound they would normally be producing has barely been heard—the changing shape of the lips alters it from **ee** to something more like **uh**.

Now the tongue is on the move again, although it doesn't have far to go—the blade moves up to close off the vocal tract almost completely by pressing up against the roof of the mouth behind the upper teeth. Suddenly the vocal cords, back down in the larynx, open up so that even though air is still flowing through them, they stop vibrating. Air from the lungs flows unimpeded through the partly open cords, and up to the front of the mouth, where it's forced to pass by the tongue. It makes a **sh** sound as it does. (Dutch and Spanish speakers find it difficult to distinguish between **sh** and **s** in English, because they don't use the two in their languages. That likely means they wouldn't hear the difference between "He shoots ... ," and "He suits ...") The **sh** sound really only differs from **s** in that it involves a much broader contact between the tongue and the roof of the mouth, and

sh contains a selection of lower pitches: **s** is strictly a high-pitched sound. If it were a musical
sound, it would be four octaves above middle C
and up.

Now the tongue has to detach itself from the
roof of Foster's mouth, and fall back quickly under
the soft palate—by doing so it narrows the air passage, just as it did at the beginning during the **ee**
sound in "he." But because it's further back in the
mouth now, the shape of the vocal tract is different, and a different sound is made: **oo**. The lips
have pretty well stayed where they were: already
rounded for **sh**, they stay rounded for the **oo**.

Now things happen quickly: Foster's tongue and
lips have to get back to where they were at the
beginning (he's coming up to another "he"), but
before they get there, there's a **ts** at the end of
"shoots" to take care of.

The tongue leaps forward in the mouth once
again and presses against the front teeth and the
gums just behind them—for the briefest of
moments, the air flow stops completely, blocked
by the tongue, and closed off by the vocal cords.
The cords suddenly re-open (but refrain from
vibrating) and an explosion of air forces its way
past the tongue, making the final **s** sound of
"shoots."

Even as the **s** is being spoken, the lips should
already be spreading out as they did for the first
"he." But if you say "He shoots he scores" to yourself quickly, you'll see that the second "he" really
doesn't have the **h** sound in it—the quiet rush of

air that would normally signal an **h** is lost completely here in the race from **s** to **ee**. "He shoots, he ..." has become "He shootsee ..." The **ee** sound is coming up, and the lips have to set up for that. However, by moving early, they cause a subtle change in the sound of the **s**: this **s** is not the same as the **s** we're about to hear in the word "scores."

Another brief touch of the tip of the tongue behind the top front teeth (**s**), and then it falls back *again*, under the soft palate, as it did for the **oo** sound, but this time it presses its back right up against the flesh of the soft palate and all air movement stops. That's **k**.

The tongue pulls away from the soft palate and bunches in the middle of the mouth to begin the **o** of "scores." It doesn't stay still though—the **o** sound requires a slow move up and back in the mouth. But not for long ... it shifts in one continuous motion from the back of the mouth up and towards the front. As that's happening, the lips pull back to the slight rounding needed for the **r**. And finally, another **s**, but not like the last **s**. That last **s** was produced with the vocal cords stilled. This time, the **s** has a buzz: "scoreszzzzzz." The vocal cords are vibrating.

How many times did Foster Hewitt utter that phrase? That one tiny phrase? And what minuscule percentage of his total verbal output was it? And remember, this was, for him, an automatic, rehearsed phrase. Next time you're having a conversation with someone, pause to think about what your vocal apparatus is having to do to produce those unique, never-before-uttered sentences that come tumbling out of your mouth one after the other, without a millisecond's consideration on your part.

Children just learning to talk have trouble with these verbal gymnastics, and so, sensibly enough, they create their own versions of difficult-to-say words.

All parents have had the experience of hearing a child pronounce a word one way when it's clear they know it should be pronounced differently. When my daughter Amelia was about two years old, she pronounced "duck" and "dark" as "guck" and "gark." Is this mispronunciation the result of her inability to pronounce the letter "d," or did she actually think the words *were* "guck" and "gark"? Easy to find out:

Jay: "Is this a guck?"

Amelia: "Guck."

J: "A guck?"

A: "No ... guck."

J: "You mean ... duck?"

A: "Yaah ... guck."

She obviously knew that the word was duck, not guck, but couldn't articulate it. Neil Smith, a linguist in England, studied the same sort of mistakes in his own children and found that these substitution errors were anything but random. The choices for replacement letters followed a strict set of rules, rules that would be forgotten completely once the child became mature enough to pronounce all the letters. One example: when the first letter in a word is a consonant requiring the tongue to press against the gums just behind the front teeth (t, d, s or z) and that sound is then followed by one requiring the tongue to move all the way back to the roof of the mouth (k, g, ng), that first letter will be changed to one that can be made at the back, thus eliminating the need to move the tongue quickly. Duck becomes "guck," doggie becomes "goggie," and ticket becomes "ckicket." Smith calculated there were thirty such rules governing his son's corruption of adult speech. The rules make sense, because they make the very tricky task of talking a little easier.

As complex as the production of Foster Hewitt's trademark four words seems to be when it's analyzed step by step, it's only the first step in communication. There were hundreds of thousands of Canadians who *heard* this phrase and understood immediately what Foster Hewitt meant. That too is a remarkable feat.

4

Now Listen and Listen Good

Each time Foster Hewitt uttered "He shoots, he scores," there was a slight difference in sound quality, tone of voice, timing and emphasis, depending on the situation. (As anyone who actually remembers Foster knows, Leaf goals inspired a certain high-pitched joyous intensity.) Yet everyone in the radio audience understood those sounds instantly, realized what had happened and probably responded with sounds of their own—all in less than a second. This is not a case of talk in the normal sense, but it does illustrate how complicated the problem of understanding human language is: a few simple words in the right setting can touch off the range of emotion from joy and relief to dismay and even despair.

If producing a simple well-practised phrase demands as many subtle commands and movements as we've seen, what must happen when you have a conversation? You can spend hours stringing together unique combinations of words, virtually error-free. But perhaps even more astounding—when you consider what's involved—is that your partner in conversation hears what you're saying, understands it and is able to respond.

Just hearing the words is tricky enough: as with all the senses, the raw material, in this case pressure waves of sound, must be converted to electrical signals before the brain can be made aware of them. Some of this translation is done even before the sound reaches the brain: in the inner ear, the to and fro of the eardrum and the trembling and twitching of the three little middle ear bones, the hammer, anvil and stirrup, are converted to the computer-like on-or-off signalling of nerve cells. In this regard all nerve cells are alike—they are monotonous in the way they carry signals. Those carrying the sounds of a cheery "hello" are indistinguishable from those informing you that you've just stubbed your toe—the difference is in their numbers, where they plug into the brain, and how they are there combined with other nerve impulses that place them in context and clarify the message.

The nerves carrying information about sound split into two soon after leaving the ear, one branch going to each side of the brain. They eventually reach the ultimate processing centre, the auditory cortex, a patch on the side of the brain behind the ear. So far, though there's been some processing and editing of the sound signals, it's largely been a case of getting the sound to the brain. What happens next is the largely mysterious process of perceiving and understanding the sound, and speech sounds are a unique example.

It's estimated that in a normal conversation we produce about four hundred words a minute. Each word contains several different sounds, and researchers have concluded that as we listen to someone talking, we must be processing between twenty and thirty different speech sounds every second. The only problem with that conclusion is that humans just can't make sense of sounds coming at them at that rate, so at first glance, understanding speech should be impossible. (But then again, the first time engineering analysis was applied to bumblebees, it is rumoured to have shown that they shouldn't be able to fly.) If you listen to a tape with a series of non-speech noises on it, you can distinguish and remember about seven of them per second—anything faster than that and you're hopelessly lost. If you make a tape of speech sounds—a series of different consonants and vowels—and play it at a rate of even twenty per second, it just sounds like a buzz. You simply cannot pick out the individual sounds. It's not like listening to a foreign language, it's like listening to no familiar sound at all. And yet in normal speech those sounds are coming at you even faster than that. What's the secret?

The answer is simple, if unexpected. When we speak, we don't just string together the sounds of speech. To say **bat**, you don't stick **b** onto **a** then add the **t**. Instead, the **b** flows into the **a** and the **a** turns itself into a **t**, without any real separation between the letters. Although it seems to sound exactly the same, the **a** in bat is different from the **a** in **can**, because your lips, teeth, tongue and palate are arriving at that **a** from different starting points. And even as that **a** is coming out of your mouth, your tongue is in flight towards the **t**. But to a listener an **a** is an **a**—there's no discernible difference between them.

It's easy to show that words are layers of letters, not series of them. The unnatural sound of the telephone number given to you by the disembodied voice at directory assistance illustrates how much greater speech is than the sum of its parts. Because this is just a series of numbers (spoken somewhat separately anyway) and not the sounds in a word, it should be easy to make it sound natural, yet it's far from that. Imagine if the voice had to produce the name of a city from vowels and consonants. This is part of the secret of why we're able to hear normal speech sounds coming at us at seemingly impossible speed. They're blended: we're hearing more than one sound at the same time. Speech is a video, not a series of snapshots.

If a tape recording is made of someone saying **bat**, you can try to separate the **b** sound from the **a** with a razor blade, simply by slicing off bits of tape, starting in the middle of the **a**, and working backwards towards the **b**. At some point, you should have shaved the entire **a** off, leaving the **b** behind. But it never happens. No matter how much you cut, there's always a trace of the **a**, until at the very end, when you've finally eliminated the

a sound altogether, you're left with a noise, an indefinable sort of pop or click; some have called it a chirp. It certainly is not a **b**. You could try going in the other direction, and cut progressively towards the **t**, and you'll end up with the same result. By the time you've rid the word of the **a** sound, you're left with something that you would never recognize as a **t**.

So there's no **b** in bat, yet we hear a **b**. The **a** in bat is made in a different way from the **a** in can, but they sound the same to us. In squeezing word sounds together so we can produce more of them every second, we've sacrificed consistency: what is supposed to be the same sound is acoustically different from word to word. But this poses absolutely no problem for understanding speech. Our brains are programmed to interpret many different sounds as signifying the same thing.

Take the word "Doody," as in " Howdy Doody." The two **d**'s sound exactly the same, but they're far from it. If you do the same trick with them on tape as with the **ba** sound above—slicing the **d** sound away as best you can from the vowel that follows —you would find that the two **d**'s not only don't sound like **d**'s any more—that much you'd expect given the example of **bat**—they also sound utterly different from each other. One, the **d** cut away from "doo," sounds like a whistle, starting low and rising in pitch. The other **d** is the reverse: a whistle that starts high and finishes low. Alone, neither sounds anything like speech, yet as parts of words we hear them as straightforward **d**'s. By the time they reach conscious awareness, your brain has analyzed the two different sounds in their contexts, defined them both as **d**'s, and that's how you hear them.

You could dissect all the sounds out of perfectly ordinary words, and you would undoubtedly succeed in proving that we are never really hearing what we think we are. The idea that many sounds that we take as being the same, like the **d**'s above, are actually quite different is remarkable enough, but there's more. The reverse is true too: speech sounds that you have no trouble distinguishing are not as different as you might have expected.

F, **th**, **s** and **sh** are four very different sounds that are rarely confused. But there are similarities: they all last the same amount of time, and they are all uttered with the vocal cords still. We distinguish them by paying attention (unconsciously) to some subtler differences. One is loudness: **s** and **sh** are louder than **f** and **th**. The loud pair can then be identified by pitch: **sh** is lower than **s**. Hearing the difference between **f** and **th** is lot trickier. Although you can, by pronouncing them over and over, convince yourself that there are huge differences between **f** and **th**, especially in the way you position your tongue and lips, the important feature of speech sounds is not how they feel to the sender but how they sound to the receiver, and in that they're much the same.

An **f** is made by pushing air through the gap between the upper teeth and the lower lip, while the air for a **th** finds its way between the tip of the tongue and the upper teeth. But in speech we don't actually hear the sound differences that result directly from the positioning of the tongue and teeth. What we hear instead are how these sounds change as lips and tongue start *moving* from the **f** or **th** sound to where they have to be for the upcoming vowels, whatever those are. You hear the beginning of the vowel, determine (again unconsciously) where the tongue and lips must have been a split second before, and conclude that they were making an **f** or a **th**.

There are very few, if any, straightforward, uncomplicated word sounds. Each one differs from sentence to sentence, even from word to word. Sounds are heard, not as they *are*, but as they were or will be. Faced with a situation as fluid as this, the brain must use whatever strategies it can to grasp what is being said. These range from applying the most rigid single criterion imaginable in defining a sound, to making flexible judgments that rely less on the sound itself than its context.

For example, your brain makes the decision about whether you've just heard the letter **b** or **p** on a completely arbitrary basis. The only difference between these sounds is in your throat. Both start with a little explosive puff of air through pursed lips, but with the **b**, your vocal cords start vibrating before or at the same time as your lips make their first sound. There is, however, a vocal cord delay with the **p**: you're making a breathy sound with your lips *before* your vocal cords start buzzing. Try holding your Adam's apple as you say both letters, and you'll feel the difference. People differ widely in the timing of that delay—it can be anywhere from ten to sixty thousandths of a second after the first puff of air, but regardless of the differences among individuals, our brains identify the letter based on that timing. If the vocal cords start twenty-five thousandths of a second or more *after* the beginning of the letter, it's deemed to be a **p**. If the delay is any less than that, it's a **b**. If your intent is to say a **b**, but there's too much of a delay before your vocal cords start to buzz, your listeners will hear a **p**.

Although the human brain has a firm rule for choosing between **b** and **p**, context may sometimes override the initial perception. In fact, on May 25, 1992, a certain CBC radio personality began her show, "Hi, I'm Figgy Gabereau" and no one even noticed. Try it yourself: the difference between Vicki and Figgy are just those differences of turning on the vocal cords early or late described above for **b** and **p**. Sometimes there's a conflict between acoustic and other evidence, and the acoustic doesn't always prevail. In one experiment someone voiced the sound **ba** while volunteers watched a person on a video mouth **va**. Most of them reported hearing **va**. Whenever sounds are indistinct, we guess what they are, based on the context: people in another experiment who heard sentences like: "Paint the fence and the _ate," where the first letter of that last word was indistinct, naturally reported hearing "gate." But when exactly the same word completed *this* sentence, "Check the calendar and the _ate," they heard "date."

One of my favourite examples of expectation and guesswork overriding the testimony of the senses was first reported more than twenty years ago. In a taped sentence like, "The premiers returned from Ottawa to their respective legislatures to report on the federal–provincial meetings" the "is" in legislatures was cut out of the tape and replaced with a cough. So the word became "leg(cough)latures." But nobody—and I've tried this myself—hears it that way. All hear the complete word "leg*is*latures," with a cough happening sometime either before or after. It's a remarkable demonstration of how our language processing equipment has developed ways of getting us successfully through the noise, omissions and general sloppiness of a normal conversation.

In trying to explain how we're able to process— at very high speed—the amount and variability of sound that passes for human speech, some scientists have suggested that we pay attention ultimately not to the sounds we hear, but to the movements that produced them. The argument is that somewhere in our brains we automatically and unconsciously match the speech sounds we hear to the lip, tongue and vocal cord movements we ourselves would make to produce those sounds. We don't actually *make* the speech movements, or even send messages to the muscles—the comparison would be done only in the brain. But it has been argued that only by reconstructing those movements can we understand what has been said. (So people who move their lips when they're reading may be, in an exaggerated way, doing what we all do to understand speech.) This may seem to be going to extremes to explain how we understand speech, but it does address the problem of dealing with the tremendous inconsistency in the sounds we hear as we listen to different people in different settings.

This theory would explain, for instance, how you can hear the two **d**'s of Howdy Doody as the same, when acoustically they're totally different. You would recognize that the acoustic differences are caused by the location of the tongue and the lips, and "understand" (unconsciously) that the intent was to produce two identical **d** sounds. One small piece of evidence that makes this theory ring true is the experiment that showed that people who saw a face mouthing the sound **va**, and at the same time heard **ba**, were certain they heard **va**. Maybe they were bypassing the actual sound and going right to the visual evidence that the sound was **va**.

This theory is by no means accepted by everyone, and indeed the solid evidence that some apes, like the chimpanzee Kanzi and the gorilla Koko, can understand spoken English (full sentences in Kanzi's case) argues against it. These animals can't speak English, so they have no brain program for producing speech to compare with the speech they hear. On the other hand, when people slated for brain surgery have their language areas marked (so that the surgeon can avoid them), scientists have sometimes found small patches of brain tissue devoted both to movements of the speech muscles and the identification of speech sounds, a finding that would square pretty well with this idea. Either way, this theory is a good example of how psychologists have had to dig deep to explain how it is that conversation comes so easy. It shouldn't, based on the speed and complexity of the speech sounds that our brains have to decode every second. But speech is completely routine for most people—that's what makes it difficult to analyze. Sometimes it takes a tragic loss of language to shed unexpected light on how we talk.

5

<<< No Ifs, Ands or Buts

In April 1861 at a meeting of the Society of Anthropology in Paris, a young surgeon, Paul Broca, reported the results of a very unusual autopsy. The deceased patient had been virtually speechless for twenty years: despite making great efforts to communicate by both speech and gesture, the only word he ever uttered was "tan." There was one exception: every once in a while, whenever the anger at not being understood overtook him, he would angrily add: "*Sacre nom de Dieu!*" The man's right side was partially paralyzed too, so his ability to communicate was restricted to gestures with his left hand. Even so, as far as Broca could tell, "Tan" (whose real name was Leborgne) was intelligent enough to be able to talk.

At the autopsy, Broca had found extensive damage to Tan's brain: large areas had virtually wasted away, so much so that the brain appeared to have lost about a third of its original weight. But the significant feature was that the origin of that damage seemed to be at the front on the left side of Tan's brain.

Later that year Broca described a second patient with speech difficulties who turned out also to have suffered damage to the left front part of his brain. Then came another—and another. Finally after eight such patients, Broca made the claim that immortalized him:

"I have been struck with the fact that the lesion always lay not only in the same part of the brain but always the same side—the left ... It seems from all this that the faculty of articulate language is localized in the left hemisphere, or at least that it depends chiefly upon that hemisphere."[9]

Broca's announcement relieved a logjam in thinking about the brain. Earlier in the nineteenth century phrenologists had made the farfetched claim that dozens of different human characteristics, including dexterity, speech, combativeness, republicanism and even "veneration of the deity," could be mapped to specific locations in the brain. But even this wasn't enough for some, and phrenology soon began to acquire a bad reputation as its more enthusiastic proponents went on to argue that you could predict the outstanding emotional or mental qualities of a person by feeling the bumps on their skull, supposedly because every bump reflected unusual growth of the brain directly underneath. The backlash that followed went so far as to deny that *any* mapping of the brain was possible, that it was a featureless, mysterious gel.

But there were lingering suspicions that some human abilities had their own locations, and that speech was one of these.

One of Paul Broca's colleagues was so sure that the phrenologists had been correct in claiming that the speech centres were at the front of the brain that he had already offered five hundred francs to anyone who could produce a post-mortem brain with significant damage at the front that had not caused its owner obvious language problems. (Too bad there isn't a little more of that now: scientists challenging their colleagues with money up front. It would make academic disputes so much more fun to watch.)

There has been a lot of controversy in the century and more since Broca's announcement. Some skeptics have taken a second look at the brains he studied and claimed that they don't exhibit the damage he claimed. Others have pointed to the fact that nearly thirty years earlier, a French doctor named Marc Dax had come to the same conclusion on the basis of forty cases of his own. But Dax's report was read only to the Congress of Physicians of Southern France, and went no further until Broca made his claims. Scholars still debate whether Broca knew about Dax before he went public.*

---

* Broca could also have been scooped by John Abercrombie, an eminent Scottish physician of the early nineteenth century. In 1836 he described forty-eight cases of language disturbances resulting from brain

Whether he overstated his case or not, Broca
pretty well had it right. In most people—more than
ninety percent—language is controlled by the left
side of the brain. That group includes virtually all
right-handers, and many left-handers too. About
fifteen percent of left-handers (that's one and a half
percent of the total population) are right-sided,
while another fifteen percent have language on
both sides.

The "sides" refer to the division of the upper
part (and vast majority) of the human brain into
right and left hemispheres, which, although they
can function independently, are normally in constant communication. The brain itself is a soggy
three-and-a-half-pound lump of tissue, about
eighty-five percent of which is water. This
explains the unsettling fact that if you take a brain
out of its skull and just leave it on the table, it will
slowly sag out of shape. (A neuroanatomist
decribed it to me as being like "chocolate pudding" although salmon mousse would be a more
appropriate colour.) At the Yakovlev collection of
human brains at the Armed Forces Pathology Lab
in Washington DC (where they have over 1600
human brains, preserved and carved into thin

---

injury, but didn't even comment on the obvious preponderance of left-side damage. He might have been
scared off by the then still heated controversy over
phrenology. (H. Forstl, "The Dilemma of Localizing
Language," *Brain and Language* 40 (1991): 145–150)

slices for easy microscopy), it takes about a year to make a brain sliceable by hardening it gradually by replacing the water in it with plastic.

Don't be misled by the fact that brains are watery: they are packed with cells, something approaching one hundred billion nerve cells or neurons, each of which is probably in communication with hundreds if not a few thousand others. If this is a computer, it's one of unparalleled capacity. Neurons are like living electrical switches—if one is stimulated strongly enough, a pulse of electricity will pass along it from one end to the other. The arrival of the pulse at the terminal of the cell causes it to dump hundreds of molecules called neurotransmitters into the narrow gap between this cell and the next. If enough of those transmitted plug into their appropriate receptors on the surface of the next cell, it too will fire. Or not: the relationship between these two cells might be one of inhibition rather than stimulation. If there are enough excitatory reactions, and enough cells talking to each other, a small initial stimulus can create a neurological domino effect. This happens all the time in the brain—when it gets out of control, you have an epileptic seizure. But even normal levels of mental activity demand that nerve cells burn lots of sugar for energy, and it's possible today to detect where in the brain glucose is being burned most rapidly, and so what areas are the most active when we are talking, thinking, listening or watching.

There aren't very many people who are able to

envision their thoughts or feelings reduced to networks of nerve cells firing off electrical signals among themselves. Most scientists have a lot of trouble imagining just how that works in detail, but most would at the same time accept that that *is* how the brain works. Even so, that's still a long way from understanding what exactly goes on in the brain when you talk. Or listen. Or have a rapid-fire conversation. For most of the twentieth century, the best way to find out where language is in the brain has been to study those unfortunate people who have lost some or all of their ability to communicate.

Thousands of Canadians have strokes every year. A typical one begins when a tiny solid clot of blood is dislodged from the crusty buildup on the inside wall of an artery, and is carried headlong by the rush of blood through the carotid artery to the brain. With every successive branch the blood vessels narrow, until suddenly the clot becomes stuck. The vessel is blocked, blood stops flowing, and the brain cells in the vicinity are starved of oxygen. The brain needs a quarter of the body's total oxygen intake, and even a few seconds of oxygen deprivation causes irreparable damage. It's still not clear exactly what causes all these cells to die: sheer lack of oxygen is enough for those in the immediate vicinity, but there is evidence that starving brain cells also release chemicals that hasten the death of their neighbours. The end is the same: a dead patch in the brain, with thousands, even millions of brain cells lost forever. They won't regrow.

Strokes can be massive and incapacitating, even fatal. They may go unnoticed. Either way, they can serve as a natural, albeit agonizing, experiment of nature. If they are on the left side of the brain, they can become an experiment with human language. Victims of such a stroke can be left with a language disability that reveals in a unique way, how the brain stores and produces language. It's cruel but true: if there weren't so many people having strokes, the understanding of language would be much more primitive than it is today. It isn't just strokes: brain tumours or head injuries can leave the victim with the same kind of localized injury, and similar specific, and sometimes very odd, language problems. And while young children and even some adults can make dramatic recoveries from these brain injuries, others are left to struggle with problems of which they are sometimes not even aware.

Paul Broca's first patient, Tan, was an extreme example of the condition now called Broca's aphasia—*aphasia* meaning the loss of speech. Tan hardly said more than four or five different words. Broca's second reported patient was no better. By now many hundreds of patients with this kind of speech problem have been studied, and while they usually can speak many more than half a dozen words, for them, speaking never comes easily—and listening to them is painful:

"Water ... man, no woman ... child ... no, man ... and girl ... oh dear ... cupboard ... man, falling ...

jar ... cakes ... head ... face ... window ... tap."[10]
This man is describing a busy kitchen scene with an overflowing sink, a boy about to topple off a stool as he reaches for the cookie jar, and a girl watching and reaching up to accept a cookie. It's part of a standard psychological test to determine the nature and severity of language loss.

"Why, yes ... Thursday, er, er, er, no, er, Friday ... Bar-ba-ra ... wife ... and, oh, car ... drive ... purnpike ... you know ... rest and ... tee-vee."[11]
That little paragraph is from another man trying to describe some of the events in his life: again, it's typical of what people with Broca's aphasia can produce. They drop the endings from verbs and nouns, and omit small parts of speech, like "of" and "and." One of the hardest things for a Broca's aphasic to say is, "No ifs, ands or buts," even though these are among the commonest words in English. Their speech is filled with concrete words, like nouns. And what they *do* produce is accomplished only with great effort. Even so there are occasional phrases—especially those the person must have used over and over—that come out suddenly and spontaneously, surprising even the speaker. Remember that Broca's original patient, Tan, used to say *"Sacre nom de Dieu!"* Howard Gardner, in his book *The Shattered Mind*, describes a patient who always stumbled painfully along, coming out with single words followed by long pauses, but was able to count to twenty and list the days of the week at normal speed. This man's inability to cope with the small connecting words

of English was striking: he could read aloud "bee" and "oar," but he had trouble with "be" and "or."

Patients with Broca's aphasia sound a little like toddlers who are just begining to speak. They understand most of what's being said to them, sometimes in precise detail, but their speech is slow and difficult.

Broca's aphasia is literally a speech loss. But damage to other language areas in the brain may have surprisingly different effects. Thirteen years after Broca's first reports, a German scientist, Carl Wernicke, identified what appeared to be a second speech centre on the left side of the brain. The effects of damage here are totally different:

"If I could I would. Oh, I'm taking the word the wrong way to say, all the barbers here whenever they stop, you it's going around and around, if you know what I mean, that is tying and tying for repucer ... repuceration, well, we were trying the best that we could while another time it was with the beds over there ..."[12]

"I felt worse because I can no longer keep in mind from the mind of the minds to keep me from mind and up to the ear which can be to find among ourselves."[13]

And in the most extreme cases:

"Eeh, oh malaty? Eeeh favility? Abelabla tay kare. Abelabla tay to po saty here. Aberdar yeste day. And then abedeyes dee, aaah, yes dee, ye ship, yeste dey es dalababela. Abla desee, abla detoasy, abla ley e porephee, tee arabek. Abla get sik?"[14]

Where someone with Broca's aphasia can hardly

get the words out, a patient with Wernicke's aphasia has no trouble getting them out at all. While you can, with patience, fill in the gaps and figure out what a Broca's patient is trying to say, Wernicke's patients are often incomprehensible. Their speech is rambling and disconnected, filled either with words that don't belong, or words that they have made up, or both. Broca's patients are usually aware that they are having difficulty speaking and being understood; Wernicke's patients don't realise there *is* a problem, even though they may have some idea that people find it hard to understand what they're saying.

If you place your finger just above your left temple, directly underneath, on the surface of the brain, there is a patch of brain tissue, a little bigger than a quarter, called Broca's area. Now move your finger back just above and slightly behind your ear. There, slightly more spread out, is Wernicke's area. The traditional view has been that if either of these parts of the brain is damaged, you will develop the appropriate language disability. The locations make sense. Broca's area, towards the front of the brain, is next door to the part of the brain that's responsible for directing the movements of the tongue and lips. You could then imagine Broca's area to be a place where precise directions for making the sounds of words are assembled, and if somehow that assembly were to be disrupted, then halting and impoverished speech could result. But as you'll soon see, that's only one small part of the picture.

Wernicke's area is further back, closer to auditory processing areas where incoming speech is processed and analyzed. It seems odd that damage there would cause someone to produce fluent but unintelligible speech, but the explanation may lie in the intimate relationship between hearing and speech. It's generally accepted that we listen to every word we say; at every moment, we're monitoring the sounds that come out of our mouths so that we can change the positions of the tongue and lips, moving from sound to sound at exactly the right pace. If you've ever tried talking while listening to a tape-delayed version of your own voice, you know how quickly your speech can disintegrate if you can't listen to it as it's coming out.*

The explanation for Wernicke's aphasics would

---

* Tongue-twisters may also illustrate the link between hearing your own voice and speaking. Some experts speculate that "The sea seetheth and it sufficeth us," or the more familiar "She sells sea shells at the seashore," are hard to say because the same or very similar sounds come up one after the other in rapid succession, and so there just isn't time to hear the sounds you're making and send the correct messages to co-ordinate the movements to produce the next sound. I'm actually not convinced by that explanation —it seems to me that "She sells sea shells" is just difficult to get your tongue around. But even if tongue-twisters do illustrate the tight connection between hearing and speaking, both they and the effects of tape delay are obviously trivial compared to the per-

be that they are somehow incapable of that auditory monitoring of what they're saying, so they produce a stream of unintelligible speech containing a wide variety of wrong words. There are, however, some recent hints that the picture may not be quite so clear. Studies using the brain-imaging technique called positron emission tomography have shown that the auditory areas of the brain are not active when we speak—just how that information can be squared with the commonly held opinion that we *do* listen as we talk isn't clear.

Sometimes the words that people with Wernicke's aphasia come out with are close to the word that's called for ("comb" instead of "hair"), sometimes they are words that have mistakes in them, and sometimes they are newly made-up words. As this stream of inappropriate words comes out, the monologue strays farther and farther from where it began.*

As long as there were thought to be two main speech areas on the left side of the brain (in most

---

manent elimination of some part of your auditory system by an injury to Wernicke's area in the brain.

* Oddly enough, although there are lots of children with aphasia, they're practically all the Broca's type. There are no reported cases I know of children with Wernicke's aphasia. It's been suggested that young children haven't yet developed the capacity for fluent speech, so even if they suffer damage to that part of the brain, they're just not yet able to produce rambling, disconnected speech.

people), the picture was straightforward. There were the two primary language deficits, Broca's and Wernicke's aphasia, and then there should be others that could be seen as variations on this theme. An example is conduction aphasia, a condition Wernicke himself predicted, where people can understand what's said to them, but they can't make a sensible reply. Their speech, like those with Wernicke's aphasia, is fluent but meaningless, and worse, they can't even repeat what they've just heard aloud. The traditional explanation has been that the brain damage is in the path from Wernicke's area to Broca's area, so they can't respond to what they've just heard because that information never gets to the area that determines what they're going to say.

Then there are cases in which the speech centres themselves remain undamaged, but become isolated from other parts of the brain that normally control them. These people are usually perfectly able to repeat what's been said to them—in fact, in extreme cases, that is all they *can* do.

But this relatively straightforward picture has disintegrated in the last decade or so. It hasn't got to the point where the guests at the psycholinguists' dinner party would sneer if you referred to Broca's and Wernicke's areas, but they would be hoping that you knew things had progressed much further. Take Broca's aphasics: they speak with a halting noun-filled speech containing few verbs and almost no small words like "and," "but," "if" or "when." Their lack of fluency has in the past been attributed to the fact that this left front part of the brain is close to the brain area responsible for programming the movement of lips and tongue for speech. But there's much more to it than that. These people do understand that the words they find difficult, the articles, pronouns and conjunctions, *are* real words, but they can't seem to dig them out of wherever they're stored and use them, or both.

Dr Helen Neville at the Salk Institute in La Jolla, California, has demonstrated dramatically that this left front part of the brain—including Broca's area —plays a crucial role in the perception and understanding of these words.[15] Neville is able to measure the electrical activity from nerve cells all over the brain when she shows a person a sentence, one word at a time, each word appearing on a screen for only a fifth of a second. At the appearance of each word, there are sudden surges in the normal electrical background in the brain.

People with normal hearing and speech experience such a surge in the left front part of the brain—Broca's area—when they see words like "but" or "when" or "if," the words that make grammatical sentences possible. That area of the brain doesn't react much when concrete words like nouns and verbs are seen, but an area at the back of the brain on both sides does. But even more interesting is what happened when Helen Neville gave these same sentences to people who had been deaf from birth, and who in grammar tests rarely do as well as hearing people. When the words "like," "and," "as," "if" and "but" appeared on the screen, the left front part of the brain remains silent. Helen Neville's experiments seem to show that we use one part of the brain for "grammar" words and another for concrete words like nouns and verbs. Damage to the "grammar" part of the left side of the brain may leave a person with Broca's aphasia, the main problem of which is a striking inability to deal with just these words.

It's not just Helen Neville's electrical recordings that show that the left front part of the brain has a special responsibility for the words that determine the structure of the sentences we speak. Imagine you're sitting in a psychology lab, and from time to time combinations of letters suddenly appear in front of you. You have to decide, as quickly as possible, whether they are words or not. It's been known for a long time that the more common a word is, the less time it takes subjects like you to decide whether it's a real word or not. But that only applies to certain words: the concrete nouns and verbs that are the real substance of conversation. The other words, the articles, conjunctions, the "ifs, ands and buts" take about the same time no matter how common they are. That suggests that somehow your brain deals with them differently. What's intriguing about this kind of experiment is that people with Broca's aphasia treat both kinds of words in exactly the same way: the more common they are, the faster they recognize them. To these people, words like "as," "and" and "if" are dealt with in exactly the same way as are "cow" or "automobile." Maybe the special system for processing these words that most of us have has been lost in Broca's aphasics: that would explain why they have trouble producing these words in the appropriate places when they talk, and also why they have trouble understanding complicated sentences like "The boy whose girl-friend owned the dog is coming into town today." Or "The bird that the cat watched was hungry." In the latter example, a Broca's aphasic shown a picture of that scene and then asked, "Who was hungry?" will most often wrongly choose what seems to be the obvious answer—the cat. Again, the problem is not in dealing with the concrete, the bird, the dog, the girlfriend or the cat, it's with the grammatical glue that holds these together in a specific relationship, words like "that" and "whose." So Broca's aphasia is far from being a simple problem of not being able to co-ordinate the production of fluent speech; it's a problem of language in the broadest sense.

In the 1990s the trend is to finer detail: trying to isolate ever-smaller areas in the brain that play some role in language; studying patients who have much more subtle language disabilities than the traditional aphasias, and using more powerful imaging techniques to watch what happens in the brain when a person hears even a single word. Taken together, these new studies are hinting that language is much less centralized than previously thought, so much so that it might make sense to think of the whole brain as making a contribution to language. It's common to talk about the left side of the brain as the "language" hemisphere, but that's more convenient than accurate. There is plenty of evidence to show that the right hemisphere understands some language, but certainly not nearly as much as the left. But it would be wrong to say it's completely uncomprehending of speech, and in fact one case in the 1970s of a woman then in her thirties illustrated just how important the right hemisphere might be in conversation and communication.[16] She'd had a stroke in her *right* hemisphere, usually a cause for relief because it means that speech has almost always been spared. Yet this woman, a teacher, had experienced a profound change in her speech: it was now devoid of emotion. Even though she could still *feel* anger, warmth or sadness, her speech remained flat and lifeless. Neurologist Elliot Ross decided this was a mirror-image case of Broca's aphasia: this woman was as incapable of colouring her speech as Broca's patients are of assembling it. Her speech had none of the rhythm, changes of pitch and stress that convey feelings as we talk. Ross soon began to uncover similar patients, some of whom were unable to express emotion (right-brain Broca's patients), and some who couldn't understand the emotions expressed by others (right-brain versions of Wernicke's aphasia).

Paul Broca and Carl Wernicke opened the door to thinking about language as belonging on the left side of the brain, and their contribution hasn't been forgotten; at the same time it's clear it's nowhere near the whole story.

6

Where Are the Words?

A bizarre case of loss of language came to light in 1985: a young man, then twenty-four, had suffered a stroke, and although he wasn't severely impaired, he kept insisting he had problems naming certain things.[17] It soon turned out these were fruits and vegetables. He could name anything else—toys, tools, body parts or kitchen items—without any problem. But when faced with line drawings, photographs or even actual fruits and vegetables, he was able to name fewer than two-thirds of them. When asked to sort seventy-five pictures of fruits, vegetables, animals, vehicles and food products into piles of the same things, his only confusion came with fruits and vegetables: he named six out of twenty-three vegetables as fruit, three of twenty-four fruits as vegetables, and also identified butter and cheese as vegetables.

It didn't matter whether he was shown the fruits and vegetables or heard visual descriptions of them, he still had trouble naming them. On the other hand, if he were told the name of the fruit out loud, he could easily match what he heard with a picture of that fruit. So he knew what they were, he recognized their names, but he couldn't produce the name himself.

This is only one of many examples that have been discovered in the last ten years or so that are starting to suggest how words are grouped together in our brains. Researchers have reported patients who can find the words to describe inanimate objects, but are lost when it comes to identifying living things and foods! Another man can name tools but not different kinds of metal, clothing but not types of cloth.

Then in February of 1991, Alfonso Caramazza and Argye Hillis reported in the science magazine *Nature* the results of studies they'd done with two female stroke victims, one sixty-two, the other forty-eight. These patients' performances on language tests revealed something even more extraordinary: we store verbs and nouns in different ways in the brain. And words that can be both verb and noun (place, move, crunch, lodge) are stored twice, once as noun, and again as verb. None of these strange claims would have been made had not these two patients come to the scientists' attention. The scientists were able to show that in some cases they have trouble with a word when it's being used as a verb, but not when it's a noun, even though it's exactly the same word!

The two women have slightly different disabilities, but they share the most striking problem: they both have trouble understanding and repeating verbs, much more trouble than they have with nouns. The problem is made most evident by giving them tests involving words that can be both noun and verb, like "fence" and "book." If these words are used as verbs (as in swordplay or reserving a table), H.W. and S.J.D. will have difficulty with them. If instead they are used to mean "a barrier around a field" or "a thing with pages and print," then they will have no problem.

Here's an example: both were dictated a sentence and then asked to write the emphasized word in the blank space in a typed sentence. So, to test nouns, a sentence dictated might be, "There's a crack in the mirror; write 'crack.'" The patient was then supposed to write "crack" in the sentence, "There's a _____ in the mirror." The same procedure would then be used for the verb. The sentence given orally was "Don't crack the nuts in here; write 'crack.'" Both H.W. and S.J.D. were then supposed to write "crack" in, "Don't _____ the nuts in here."

The second version of the test was to give them the sentences to read to themselves, then ask that they pronounce the word "crack." The test was done in these two ways, written and spoken, because the two women differ in their abilities to deal with words that they see and words that they hear. But the bottom line was that while both H.W. and S.J.D. had little trouble with words like "crack" as nouns, they scored only about fifty percent right when those same words were used as verbs!

The presumption here is that the strokes suffered by these two women probably killed the cells in some small areas of their brains. As a result, they have lost the ability either to write or to speak verbs that they have just heard or read. Yet they have no problem with reproducing *exactly the same word* as long as it's being used as a noun.

The conclusion has to be that we somehow store nouns and verbs in different places (or at least in different ways) in our brains, and for ambiguous words like "crack," "fence," "book," "store" and hundreds of others, we have at least two storage places.

The story of H.W. and S.J.D. is not the first evidence that our brains treat nouns and verbs differently, but what do cases like this mean? Studies in the 1930s suggested that college students knew on average more than 150,000 different words, with the maximum somewhere near 200,000, and the minimum around 100,000. These numbers have been criticized since as being too high (probably by someone who's heard college students in conversation), but even if the average number is much less, like 50,000, that's still a lot of words. Getting at them when you want to, with the speed that you need when talking, makes it difficult to imagine that words are stored in as simple an arrangement as a series of tiny compartments, each of which is a bin with the names of animals, birds or fruits, and nouns, verbs and other parts of speech.

Yet how else do you explain the man who can't name fruits and vegetables? And then when you take into account the fact that there have been other patients whose inability to name things is more extensive, and may for example cover *all* food items, then it would make sense to think of the smallest bins (fruit and vegetables) being grouped together to make a larger bin (food items), which in turn is grouped with others to make an even larger one (maybe living things and food—the living and the formerly living). Only when these patients' brains are studied at autopsy will it be possible to say with any certainty how much brain tissue was destroyed in their stroke, and where it was. And even then, it will be impossible to say very much: there are likely individual differences, and one person's produce department might not be in the same place as someone else's.

A professor of linguistics at McGill University, Dr Michel Paradis, has complicated this mystery that needed no further complications by finding bilingual patients who, after a stroke or similar event in the brain, regain only one of their original languages—and not necessarily the one in which they were most fluent—or even stranger, regain first one language, then lose it for a while and get the other one back, then switch back again.[18] This can go on for days, or even weeks. One of Dr Paradis's patients was a young man whose first language was French, and who was married to a unilingual French-speaking woman. For the first week after surgery he could speak only English, and his father had to translate for his wife. The next week he lost his English, and couldn't speak to the nurses on the ward. There are even stranger cases in the medical literature involving patients who spoke three or even four languages and lost one or more in shifting combinations as time went on. The curious thing about Michel Paradis's cases —if it isn't curious enough that you can lose one language, and not the other, then switch—is that even when his patients couldn't speak one of their languages, they could still translate into that language from the one that was working. So it wasn't a question of being unable to mouth the words, they just couldn't speak them spontaneously!

And is there some sort of explanation for these cases? Not really, although what they do illustrate is that in some way first and second (or even third) languages are kept separate and distinct in the brain, with the result that some very specific damage can take out one and not the other. Dr Paradis speculates that the switching back and forth might be understandable in terms of some sort of inhibition that can be switched on and off. You'd need that in everyday conversation: when you're speaking French, you want to switch off the English. Maybe in the early stages of recovery these patients had lost control of that switch.

The fascinating question remains, where are all these words stored? Is there some tiny circuit of neurons in your brain for aardvark or Studebaker? Is "hello" in a different place from "bonjour"? The renowned Canadian neurosurgeon Wilder Penfield pioneered a way of mapping the brain to locate exactly where the language centres on the surface were.[19] Through the 1930s and 1940s, Penfield and his team at the Montreal Neurological Institute were using surgery to help patients who were having severe, debilitating epileptic attacks. When all else had failed, surgeons like Penfield literally carved out the "hot spot," the piece of the brain where the seizures started. It may sound unnecessarily drastic, even unbelievable, but these were patients whose lives were miserable already, and they were willing to trade relief from severe and frequent seizures for what had to be an unknown life with a piece of their brain removed.

There were many risks: the operation might not relieve the epilepsy. Worse, even if the epilepsy were cured, if the surgeon cut in the wrong place, the patient could be left speechless or unable to comprehend speech. To avoid this, the surgical team had to map the speech areas in the patient's brain, which could then be avoided during surgery. But the way this was done is absolutely incredible to contemplate. Penfield and his team would actually saw through the skull and fold back a big flap of bone, bigger in area than a credit card, exposing the brain with its membranous covering, the dura mater. Then they'd slice through the dura and peel *it* back, exposing the actual surface of the brain. It was right there, exposed to the air. Meanwhile the patient was completely conscious and lucid!* He would have had only a local anaesthetic to kill the pain of the removal of the skull flap. What's more, he'd be in conversation with one of the medical staff, who would show him objects, or pictures of objects, and ask him to name them, or ask the patient to repeat phrases like "The Third Riding Artillery Brigade" or "Methodist Episcopal."

At the same time, Dr Penfield would be wielding an electrode like a pen, lightly touching the surface of the patient's exposed brain and delivering a weak electric current. If the current disrupted speech in any way, a tiny square of sterile paper with a number on it was dropped gently onto that part of the brain. After fifteen minutes of this, the doctors had a map of language, outlined by clusters of little white paper squares. Each square represented a tiny patch of brain tissue that, when

---

* If you think this scene is somewhat bizarre, consider this: Hermann Boerhaave, a famous eighteenth-century physician, reported seeing a beggar in Paris who held the top of his skull in his outstretched hand to hold the money he was given. Apparently he'd had surgery which involved the removal of his skullcap, and it had never been replaced. For an extra sum he'd allow some street neurosurgery. Donors could press gradually on his brain, harder and harder—at first he'd see stars, then lose his sight altogether, then finally lose consciousness. After the pressure was relieved, he'd gradually return to normalcy. A man who used his head.

touched by the electrode, caused the patient to be struck speechless, or to slur his words, hesitate, repeat words, or to become suddenly unable to find the name for the object at which he was looking. They would then avoid those areas during surgery.

After countless mappings like this, Penfield identified two main areas on the left side of the brain that he found were responsible for speech. One was about midway behind the left eye and ear, above the temple: that would be the twentieth-century version of Broca's area. The other, about twice as big, was behind the ear, extending both up and back from it. The total brain surface involved in these two might amount to about a quarter of the whole left side of the brain. Penfield's work was a dramatic confirmation of what people like Paul Broca had suggested, but it was so much more substantial. He wasn't poring over a damaged brain soaked in formaldehyde ... he was touching the living brain, and hearing the person say, as he looked at a foot, "Oh I know what it is. That is what you put in your shoes." Then, but only when the electrode was removed: "Foot."

Wilder Penfield published his findings in a book in 1959. In the last few years, George Ojemann, a neurosurgeon at the University of Washington in Seattle, has been doing his own electrical mapping of language areas in the brain, and he's added some curious and unexpected new twists to Penfield's work.[20] Ojemann has found that every patient's language area is different—dramatically different. One out of every five patients showed no change at all in their language ability when the electrode was placed right in Broca's area, that part of the brain that has for a hundred years been believed to be crucial for talking and understanding. Wernicke's area, the other well-known language site on the left side of the brain, fared even worse. More than two-thirds of Ojemann's patients had no language areas at all that responded to the electrode in what should have been Wernicke's area. However, many patients *did* have language-sensitive spots in these two areas—it just shows how variable the picture is.*

The other revelation from Ojemann's work is the precision with which he can point to a piece of the brain that deals with language, and how that piece can be surrounded by pieces that don't. He's been able to show that when the electrode touches one place that's less than half a centimetre across —smaller than the hole in a three-ring binder— that patient is suddenly unable to name objects. Yet clustered around on all sides are similar sized

---

* Imaging technologies like PET (positron emission tomography) have shown that when people are doing linguistic thinking, like making verbs out of nouns, there's heightened activity even in the cerebellum, a somewhat separate part of the brain at the back that, while amounting to about ten percent of the total volume of the brain, is usually thought to be responsible for controlling movement!

patches of brain that apparently have nothing to do with language at all. And there's a kind of landscape effect too. The surface of the brain, the cerebral cortex, is deeply folded, a little like an accordion, except that the pleats in the brain are soft, rounded and pinky-grey. An odd accordion. George Ojemann finds that the language areas are almost always at the surface of these folds, never in the valleys between, even though about *half* of the total surface brain tissue in this area is buried.

So if you could take the entire left cerebral cortex and smooth out the folds, the language areas would run only in narrow lines, on what had been the crests of the hills. And even in those lines, the language areas would be scattered: not intensely concentrated like the lights of the Toronto–Hamilton corridor, but more like a countryside dotted with towns, some clustered together, some off by themselves. And everyone's brain would produce a slightly different pattern. Whether these are the places where words or parts of words are kept, no one knows.

George Ojemann's probings even suggest a partial explanation for the loss of one language or the other in the bilingual patients studied by Michel Paradis and others. Ojemann has found that the areas of the brain for naming things in a second language tend to be bigger than those used for the native language, although other research has shown that both languages tend to be on the left side of the brain.

The lesson from these probings of the brain is

that it is a gross oversimplification to think that the brain has two language areas, Broca's and Wernicke's, and that between them they run the entire language program. The more probing is done, the cloudier the picture gets. George Ojemann finds unusual patterns on the surface of the brain, and techniques for imaging the interior show that language disturbances may have very deep roots—even down to what has always been considered the ancient or "reptilian" brain.

Unfortunately, as far as I know, no mapping of the brain in the way Penfield and Ojemann have done it has ever revealed a specific area that might correlate with the disabilities suffered by the stroke victims: no touch of the electrode has eliminated the ability to name fruits and vegetables, or to wipe out the understanding of verbs but not nouns. This isn't really surprising, given that you can't stand there all day giving verbal tests to a patient whose brain is exposed. If you could, who knows what you'd discover? But imaging and electrical probing will never give the whole picture—sometimes it pays off just to listen to people talk, and note the little clues about the brain that creep —unnoticed—into conversation.

7

Tongue Slips and Tongue Tips

One of the great things about language is that even without all the brain scans and electrical probes, or all the tragic albeit fascinating case histories of people who've suffered strokes and had their speech disrupted, you can do your own investigation of speech by listening to the mistakes that crop up in everyday conversation. Making a "slip of the tongue" or having something on the "tip of your tongue" are perfect examples.

The Reverend William A. Spooner was dean and warden of New College, Oxford. He died in 1930, leaving behind a long list of very funny speech errors now known as spoonerisms. Out of Spooner's mouth were supposed to have come "the queer old dean" instead of "the dear old queen." Farmers, the "noble sons of toil" became "noble tons of soil." When showing one of his parishioners to her seat for the morning service, Spooner is said to have asked, "Mardon me,

Padam, this pie is occupewed. May I sew you to a sheet?" And my favourite is this reprimand of one of his students:

"You have hissed all my mystery lectures. I saw you fight a liar in the back quad; in fact, you have tasted the whole worm."

Sadly, it's now thought to be very doubtful that Spooner actually uttered these words inadvertently, if at all. They might have been the Reverend's idea of clever humour, or more likely, the best ones were simply made up by others and attributed to him. But to be in the position of having clever word transpositions named after him must mean that William Spooner actually did make this kind of word slip often enough.* A tentative medical diagnosis of his problem suggested that he was halfway between those who make ordinary slips of the tongue and those with overt language disability. The truth is that most of us have made this sort of slip of the tongue from time to time, and they're

---

* Something that is well documented is Spooner's mixing up, not syllables, but ideas: "Poor soul ... very sad. Her late husband, you know, a very sad death—eaten by missionaries—poor soul." He also was seen committing a physical, rather than verbal Spoonerism. Having overturned a salt shaker at the dinner table, Spooner proceeded to pour red wine on it, drop by drop, until he created the little purple mound he would have had in the normal sequence of events: spilling the wine first then mopping it up with the salt.

good for much more than just a few laughs: they reveal something very interesting about talk, and how it's stored in the brain.

Words appear not to be filed away as unbreakable solid entities—little peas that are strung together to make sentences. They can be split apart and put back together in different ways.

Thousands of tongue-slips have been collected, and many of those demonstrate just how easily parts of words can be moved around—"Yew Nork" for "New York," "budbegs" instead of "bedbugs" and the legendary (if apocryphal) "This is the Canadian Broadcorping Castration." My wife, Cynthia, entered a department store in Singapore looking for something to secure her suitcase, and asked a store clerk, "Excuse me, do you smell sall locks?" (We've always thought it should be Saul Lox.)

A close look at these slips reveals not only that words can be broken up into their parts and those parts moved around, but also that those movements are not random or disorganized. For instance, the nonwords created by slips of the tongue never violate the rules of English. You can have the phrase "slips of the tongue" come out as "stips of the lung" but not as "tlips of the sung," because you can't start a word in English with "tl." Mistakes can be made, but only certain kinds of mistakes: you can come out with a nonword, but not complete gibberish.

Slips of the tongue involve much more than just switching letters or syllables between words.

Sometimes one word is substituted for another ("brouse" instead of "blouse"), or two words are squeezed into one ("spot in my heart" becomes "spart"). They can be as complicated as slips which take consonants from a later word and attach them to an earlier: cu*ff* of co*ff*ee. They can be simple reversals of words: my wife, Cynthia, describing how she was able to fall asleep on the couch: "Amelia was on my *warm*, and she was *lap*." Slips like that suggest that the sentences we speak are pre-assembled in our minds before they actually come out of our mouths. When Cynthia said, "Amelia was on my *warm*," it's obvious that the rest of the sentence was already in place ready to go.

But maybe the most interesting aspect of these spoonerisms and other slips of the tongue is that they come about as close as you can get to identifying the smallest pieces of words that we store in the brain. If you can come out with "chee cane" instead of "key chain," does that say that somewhere in the tens of billions of nerve cells in your brain there's a cluster of those cells that store the sound **ch**? Is there another for **k**? Is that the only way you could misplace them? Logic tells you that it wouldn't really make sense to have a separate storage for the words "walk," "walked," "walking" and "walker," when you could just keep "walk" and have the other additional sounds ready to add, not only to this word, but to any other that might need them.

And when you look at a slip like "glear plue

sky" instead of "clear blue sky," you're getting about as fine as you can, The **c** sound in clear is made without air vibrating through the voice-box, but it's replaced by a **g** sound that requires the voice-box. It's possible that errors like this are just mistakes in execution, but they may also be showing us that the words we utter are being assembled from the simplest of word fragments.

One of the newest theories that tries to put all the information from stroke patients and brain mapping together in the same picture suggests that words might even be stored as their individual sounds. Drs Antonio and Hannah Damasio of the University of Iowa argue that the brain uses what they call "convergence zones" to recognize objects and be aware of them.[21] So seeing a familiar face would trigger connections between the visual image of that face as well as general information about shapes, faces and people you know. These disparate pieces of information would all be turned on at the same moment, allowing you to recognize the face.

The same would hold true for a word like "cup." Antonio Damasio uses the example of thinking about a styrofoam cup: when you do, you put together information you've stored about its physical attributes like size, colour, texture and shape, and at the same time pull together the sounds **c**, **uh** and **p**. One intriguing piece of evidence that we store the characteristics of something like a cup in different places in our brains is the fact that people with severe problems in naming and recognizing objects, who when shown a cup cannot name it, say what it's for, or even describe it, can still do exactly the right thing with it: bring it to their lips. They can call up some of the features of "cup" but not all. This doesn't prove, however, that they're storing the word "cup" as its individual letters, and I think the scientific jury is still out on the claim that each individual sound in a word like "cup" is stored separately. You'd need many fewer storage places doing it that way, but more time to assemble each word from its component sounds.

Slips of the tongue may also reveal much more than how words are stored or sentences assembled in the brain. Freud—naturally—saw slips of the tongue as, well, Freudian. To him they revealed our anxieties and hidden motives. This idea has been very difficult to demonstrate convincingly, even though there have been plenty of slips collected that suggest something is on the slip-maker's mind.

Linguist Archibald Hill collected slips of the tongue that convinced him that "taboo" words play an important role in producing tongue-slips.[22] He's recorded such elaborate transformations as "broke the crystal on my watch" becoming "broke the whistle on my crotch," "don't take this as a rejection on my part" to "don't take this as an erection on my part" (one can only dream of the cartoon to match that caption), and "White Anglo-Saxon Protestant" becoming "White Anglo-Saxon prostitute." You'll note these are not mistakes in piecing words together—instead, they're mistakes of choice: the wrong word replaces the right one. It's easy to believe that choice could be influenced by what's on one's mind, but it's difficult to know exactly what these particular errors mean without knowing the context in which they were spoken.

Michael Motley at the University of California at Davis has performed some clever experiments to see if the social setting can indeed influence slips of the tongue.[23] Motley's subjects (undergraduate males) sat in front of a screen and watched as pairs of words were flashed on momentarily. They were told to read the words *to themselves*, unless they heard a buzzer, in which case they were to say them out loud. In an effort to generate enough slips of the tongue to make the experiment worthwhile, the two or three pairs preceding the one to be read out had some of the same syllables already moved around. So for instance, as Motley has pointed out, the chance that someone might misread "fruit fly" as "fluit fry" is enhanced by having them see "flat frog" and "flying froth" first.

That's the set-up that's likely to produce more tongue-slips. Then Motley designed an experiment to try to generate some true Freudian slips. In one version, volunteers were told that dummy electrodes attached to them would give them, at some unpredictable point in the experiment, a severe electric shock. In another, a "provocatively dressed" woman ran the experiment. The third version was neutral, and all three groups were given the same pairs of words to read.

The results were amazing. Under threat of elec-
trocution, subjects produced the following tongue-
slips more often than any others: "damn shock" for
"sham dock," "carried volts" instead of "varied
colts," and "cursed wattage" rather than "worst
cottage." In the presence of the woman dressed in
non-standard psychologist's garb, "fast passion"
came out instead as "past fashion," and "bare
shoulders" for "share boulders." (It's only fair to
point out that these experiments were done in the
early 1980s—I'm sure experimenters would be
much less likely today to design an experiment to
encourage undergraduate males to produce
sexually oriented slips of the tongue in the presence of a female experimenter.)

The experiment worked in the sense that these
"designed" slips were more common (occurring
more than thirty percent of the time) than others
that seemed not to have been influenced by the
setting (less than twenty percent), but the fact that
there were so many other kinds of slips underlines
the difficulty in investigating language by looking
at natural errors like slips of the tongue. There are
many different kinds of slips: some influenced by
unexpressed feelings and motivations, some by
unrelated factors, like fatigue or lack of interest,
and many which have no identifiable cause at all.
The trick is to find those that actually reveal something about the language in our brains.

There are laboratory experiments that have not
only supported the idea that it's parts of words, or
syllables, that are stored in the brain, but have also

pointed to the left hemisphere as the place where they're stored.[24] One such study made use of cleverly designed nonwords (like the experiment in Chapter Five showing how people with Broca's aphasia are different from the rest of us). Sometimes the nonwords were combinations of real parts of words (like "walken"), but sometimes not ("etrict"). But even nonsense words like "etrict" weren't just randomly assembled: they were made by changing just one letter from a legitimate word ("strict—etrict"). In a lab, it's possible to send words like this directly to one hemisphere of the brain or the other by flashing them briefly on a screen to the left or right of a point at which the subject is staring.

That's what was done in this case, and the subjects were supposed to press keys to indicate whether they thought they were looking at a word or a nonword, and to make that decision as fast as possible. As expected, the left hemisphere was much better at judging words than the right, but more interestingly, the left hemisphere (the speech side of the brain) made many more errors when the nonwords were combinations of parts of real words than when they were just nonwords, period. The right hemisphere, not very good at words to begin with, didn't seem to recognize when a nonword had real parts or not. The scientists who performed the experiment interpreted these results to mean that the left hemisphere stores the parts of words, and when it's faced with a nonword that nonetheless contains real parts it is momentarily

confused: is this a word or not? It has no such
trouble with words that don't contain real word
parts.

In 1966, psychologists Roger Brown and David
McNeill, who were then at Harvard, performed a
classic experiment on the "tip of the tongue" phenomenon.[25] We've all agonized over not quite
being able to say a name or a word that we're sure
we know, but Brown and McNeill were the first to
investigate it, and in the process, they discovered
some unexpected ways in which we remember
words, including what is now called the "bathtub
phenomenon."

The experiments were straightforward. They
chose forty-nine words that are relatively infre-
quent: they occur less than once in a million
words, but at least once, on average, every four
million. These were words like apse, ambergris,
nepotism, sampan, and cloaca: words that you
might recognize but wouldn't normally use in
everyday conversation. The experimenters read
out a definition of one of these words; students
who felt sure that they knew the word, but just
couldn't think of it at the moment, were asked to
start filling out a sheet listing what they thought
might be the number of syllables in the suspected
word, its first letter, words of similar sound and
words of similar meaning.

The results show that the tip of the tongue phenomenon is real: students who couldn't quite
come up with the word nonetheless revealed that
they knew a lot about it. When the unknown word

was one, two or three syllables, the students who held it on the tip of the tongue were very good at guessing that number: for example, when the word they were guessing was three syllables, two out of three guessed right. Fifty-seven percent guessed the first letter correctly, which is very impressive given the number of letters that *could* be first. Words that the students guessed to be similar sounding tended to have the same number of syllables as the mystery word, but words they indicated as similar only in meaning had, as you'd expect, not much resemblance to the word that was on the tip of their tongue.

The most interesting discovery was the "bathtub" effect: the beginnings and endings of words are remembered better than the middles. This is supposed to conjure up the image of someone slumped in the bathtub with his head sticking up at one end, and his feet at the other. Letter-by-letter comparisons of words judged to be similar-sounding to the actual target words made it clear that the middle letters matched least well.

This experiment, as old as it is, seems to have discovered a system for recalling words that's a little like the modern "convergence zones" put forward by the Damasios at the University of Iowa. They argue that a word is represented by many different features simultaneously: this experiment shows that, given a definition of an uncommon word, it's often the case that we can bring together many different pieces of information about it—its length, first and last letters, even retrieve from memory other words that sound the same—yet still be unable to get the word itself. We can complete part of the task of bringing together the different attributes of the word, but we fall just short. In a way, when we're having a tip-of-the-tongue experience, we must be getting a very mild taste of what it's like to see a cup, be unable to name it, describe it or say what it's for, but still be able to lift it to the lips.

When you put all of this evidence together, from lab experiments to slips of the tongue to having a tip-of-the-tongue experience, you come up with the impression that somewhere, probably in the left hemisphere, we store the parts of the words we use in everyday conversation. Nobody can yet say categorically how small those parts are, or whether there might in some cases be whole words or even phrases held intact. Regardless, it's an incredibly powerful storage system—there have been estimates that the average high-school graduate knows something like fifty to sixty thousand words. If that's true, then that person has been learning new words at an average rate of ten a day since attaining language. And you can continue to learn new words until you die.

8

And a Hearty Hi-O Argentum

Tod kekluwos owis agrom ebhuget. (... On hearing this the sheep fled into the plain.)

That is the final climactic line from a folk tale written in a language that nobody has ever heard spoken or seen written, because it disappeared thousands of years ago. But half the people in the world today speak a language that can be traced back to this extinct one. The language of the folk tale is called Proto-Indo-European, or PIE. It's the language that ultimately gave rise to every language spoken in Europe except Finnish, Hungarian, Basque and Estonian. Indo-European languages are also found in a swath from eastern Turkey through Iraq, Iran, Afghanistan, Pakistan and India to Bangladesh. There even used to be an outpost Indo-European language spoken in what is now western China. When you consider how languages like French, English and Portuguese were spread by colonization, it's no wonder that every second person on earth speaks an Indo-European language.

But if it died out thousands of years ago, how can something like that folk tale be written in Proto-Indo-European? This ancient language has been reconstructed from its descendants: linguists can look at Indo-European languages around today, add some that may be extinct but are still pretty well known, like ancient Greek and Latin, and using some rules that govern how sounds in one language change into slightly different sounds in another, can run the clock back and come up with something that they're pretty sure is close to the original Indo-European language. Although linguists seem to fight about almost everything, most agree that there were people speaking PIE a few thousand years ago. But who were they, where did they live, and when? Nobody agrees on those crucial questions, and they are what make historical linguistics—the otherwise dry and practically arcane renderings of linguistic symbols, and syllable-by-syllable analysis of languages like Sanskrit and Gothic—into something that's almost, well, romantic and exciting. Piecing together what the ancient Proto-Indo-European language must have been like has been a piece of detective work assembled over nearly two centuries, and in building up the language—from literally nothing—linguists have at the same time started to paint a picture of vast populations of farmers, hunters and conquering horsemen moving in huge migrations over the Russian steppes and through the forests of Europe and Asia thousands of years ago.

The methods used to uncover an extinct language can be described in pretty straightforward terms: you begin by searching in modern languages for words that are similar in sound and meaning. So the German word *hand*, the Dutch *hand*, the Swedish *hand*, the Danish *haand* and the word *handus* in the long-extinct Gothic, all meaning the thing at the end of your arm, are a pretty clear indication that there was an earlier word, like *hand*, that has come down to all these languages. But you have to be on your guard: you can be thrown off by coincidence, and more important, by borrowing. What if the word actually began with the Gothic, and was borrowed from that language by all the others? If that's possible, then you can't use *hand* to infer the existence of a language ancestral to all those you examined. Does the fact that you can find the word "Coca-Cola" in many European and Asian languages today mean that the Proto-Indo-Europeans were drinking and talking about a beverage with a name like that?

Linguists have ways of trying to determine that this is not what has happened. One of them is to look primarily at words for basic items in our everyday vocabulary, like body parts and numbers: they're unlikely to be borrowed, because every language would have words for them already. And while a few words might be borrowed, the case for descent from an earlier language is strengthened by numbers: the more common words you find among the modern offspring, the more likely it is that they came from an earlier source. It's also sometimes possible to recognize borrowed words: "skill," "egg," "ugly" and "keel" were all originally Norse words, and even if you're not a language expert you can see that they use pairs of letters together and lots of hard consonants like **k** and **g**, arrangements of letters characteristic of Old Norse, the language that gave rise to modern Danish, Swedish and Norwegian.

Don't think by this brief description that reconstructing dead languages is easy. All languages change virtually day to day, and when it comes to centuries of change, even the *same* language evolves to become unrecognizable. Today, we recite:

> "The Lord is my shepherd I shall not want. He maketh me to lie down in green pastures. He leadeth me beside the still waters."

In fact even that version is a little on the archaic side. But a thousand years ago, that same passage read:

> "Drihten me raet ne byth me nanes godes wan
> And he me geset on swythe good feoland
> And fedde me be waetera stathum."

Likewise for the Lord's Prayer. Six hundred years ago:

> "Oure fadir that art in heuenes
> halwid be thei name.

A thousand years ago:

> Faeder ure thu the eart on heofonum di thn
> nama gehalgod."

In 1786, William Jones, an Englishman and

Chief Justice of India, and a brilliant amateur linguist, ignited interest in the idea of a long-dead ancestor to modern languages by noting that Sanskrit, the ancient religious language of India, had strong similarities to Latin, Greek, even Gothic and Celtic. Jones had only begun to study Sanskrit three years earlier, but he had quickly concluded that there once was a language that gave rise to it, all the others listed above, and probably Persian too. In 1822 Jacob Grimm, of Snow White and Cinderella fame, contributed to the search for PIE by establishing rules by which words change as they pass from one language to the next. For instance, he showed that Latin p's become f's in the Germanic group of languages that includes English: *plenum* becomes "full," *piscis* becomes "fish," *pes* becomes "foot." Rules like those Grimm enunciated made it possible to see relationships among words that at first glance looked completely different. By comparing a wide variety of related words, taken from as many modern Indo-European languages as possible, linguists were slowly able to guess not only what the Proto-Indo-European words (the original words that led to all of the others) must have been, but even what they sounded like. Take for instance the French, Italian and Spanish words for milk: *lait*, *latte* and *leche*. Using rules like Grimm's, which set limits on how sounds can and do change with time, you would likely come up with an ancestral word *lacte*. This is a sneaky example, because the ancestral word is already known: the Latin *lactem*. But this is how the process of reconstructing ancient languages can work, as long as those doing it are always on the lookout for borrowed or invented words.

Grimm and Jones are two of the heroes of this story, but my favourite is a French linguist named Ferdinand de Saussure. In the late nineteenth century he made the bold claim that Proto-Indo-European must have contained a group of sounds that had failed to survive in any of the languages descended from it. In studying the sounds of Greek and Sanskrit he came across some vowel sounds that didn't make any sense. There was a peculiar timbre or colour to them, yet there seemed to be no good reason why there should be. They didn't seem to follow any of the rules of sound shifts like Grimm's Law. Saussure decided these strange vowel sounds were there because in Proto-Indo-European they had come immediately after a sound that now no longer existed. These extinct sounds are today called "laryngeals." Laryngeals can be heard in some modern languages, like Arabic, but they've disappeared from the Indo-European languages. They're like the sound of the letter **h**, made either with or without the vocal cords vibrating. If they are vibrating, the laryngeal sounds a bit like you're trying to clear your throat with your mouth open: they're down-in-the-throat sounds. Saussure never lived to prove his point, but in the 1920s when archaeologists unearthed some stone tablets from the archives of kings at Hattusas (in what is now Turkey), some of them turned out to be written in Hittite, a previously unknown language with no known descendants. It's an ancient Indo-European language, and on those tablets were markings for these laryngeal sounds in exactly the places within words where Saussure had suggested something odd would be found.

The folk tale referred to at the beginning of this chapter wasn't found inscribed on a stone tablet: no direct trace of Proto-Indo-European has ever been found. It was written in the middle of the nineteenth century by August Schleicher, one of the first linguists who tried to re-create PIE. It's called *The Sheep and the Horses*, and in it both animals lament the other's being used by their human masters. It's not exactly an epic, but the fact that anyone could write anything in a long-dead tongue demonstrates the power of the techniques of linguistic reconstruction.

There's little disagreement that there was once a language we today call Proto-Indo-European. But the sparks begin to fly when the questions of who spoke it and where come up.[26] In the 1930s this became much more than an academic question. The Nazis thought the idea of a Northern European homeland for the Proto-Indo-Europeans—as suggested by the Australian archaeologist Gordon Childe—was a perfect fit to their concept of a master race, much to Childe's dismay. In 1926 he had written a book called *The Aryans* (using the term as a linguist of the time would for the people who spoke the ancestral Indo-European language), and in the last paragraph of that book he wrote:

"The physical qualities of that stock did enable them by the bare fact of physical strength to conquer even more advanced peoples ... the Nordics' superiority in physique fitted them to be the vehicles of a superior language."

Hitler's Nazis exploited these ideas to the full, and Childe, demoralized by how he had been used, never again referred to his book, which was actually anything but a racist document. (Childe used "Aryan" as we would use "Indo-European," which would make Yiddish, a Hebrew-flavoured version of German, an "Aryan" language!) And the idea that that the speakers of PIE were blond, blue-eyed Scandinavian conquerors was just one of many speculations about this ancient culture. There were some wild ones too: one linguist put the Indo-Europeans at the North Pole, and an Icelandic scholar thought he heard bird calls in the sounds of PIE, and concluded they must have lived on the shores of the Baltic Sea, because that's where you can hear such natural sounds the best!

The picture is very different today. Just before I started writing this chapter I finally found a book that I had been searching for, called *Proto-Indo-European Trees*, written by Paul Friedrich. Only in the business of bringing dead languages back to life could a book like this be written: it's a 188-page discussion of all the trees, and nothing but the trees, with which the hypothetical group of prehistoric people who spoke Proto-Indo-European were familiar. Trees are included in this list if similar words for the same species appear in several of the languages known to have come down from the original. What's exciting about this sort of analysis is that if you know what trees they knew, and you know where those trees grow, you might just be able to place these people on a map.

There are, in PIE, anywhere from three to eighteen different kinds of trees. The one that seems least ambiguous is birch: a word for birch that seems to go back to PIE appears in at least six different groups of languages today. Willow is a common word, possibly because it's pliable and was useful for making baskets. Elm, too, appears to have been known to the Proto-Indo-Europeans, and ash is mentioned frequently in languages derived from PIE, often as a useful material for spear shafts (for instance, in Homer's Greek). Unfortunately those trees aren't much help in placing the ancient people who spoke this language. All of them grow widely across Europe, Asia Minor, even to Siberia.

If you just look at the European branch of this language family, there are all kinds of trees that aren't mentioned in the Asian languages: juniper, poplar, apple, maple, alder, hazel and cherry. This doesn't help much either, because two things could have happened: either the original Proto-Indo-Europeans lived in heavily forested Europe and talked about all those trees, and then those who emigrated to Asia forgot the words because the trees weren't there, or the Europeans could have invented all those words upon their arrival in Europe from an original homeland in Asia. The author of *Proto-Indo-European Trees* is content to place the people of that time in an area "rich in virgin forests, meadow groves, and wooded riversides" without being specific as to exactly where that was.

But they talked about much more than just trees. They knew plains and mountains, rivers and lakes. They talked about winter, spring and summer, but oddly enough, not fall. It was hot and cold, and there was snow and ice. And animals! Otter, beaver, wolf, bear, lynx and elk—and birds like geese, cranes, ducks and eagles. And it's not just their natural environment we know about: they raised cattle, produced butter and cheese, and used the yoke and the plough in the *agros* (field). They had oxen, goats, sheep and pigs, they spun and wove cloth from wool, and made pots from clay.* They had debts and laws (and undoubtedly lawyers), kings, and gods (their word *deiwos* became *Zeus* in Greek and *deity* in English). Some of the words in PIE have clear and obvious links to modern English, like *nepots*, meaning grandson or sister's son, which of course has become "nepotism"; some

---

* The Proto-Indo-European word for pig was *su*—it's the root of the English "swine." Every Saturday afternoon in the autumn, crazed fans of the Arkansas University football team, the Razorbacks, chant their team's cheer: "Soooooooeeeeeee pig!" That's also how hog callers attract the little porkers. So how is it that in the late twentieth century these people are chanting a Proto-Indo-European word?

show up in other modern languages: *laksos* for salmon is now "lox." A rich vocabulary * but a disappointing one: the homeland of the speakers of PIE could still be virtually any place except in the middle of treeless plains. The proof of the uncertainty is in the pudding: since the 1960s, there have been at least thirteen different places suggested by linguists as the homeland of the people who spoke Proto-Indo-European.

In the late 1980s, an archaeologist at Cambridge University, Colin Renfrew, added fuel to the fire by questioning one of the cherished beliefs about the Proto-Indo-Europeans: the idea that they spread their language across Europe and Asia as they themselves swept across the land in vast migrations, or more accurately, invasions. They have been conventionally viewed as a people who rode on horseback (out of wherever it was they lived) and conquered large populations of indigenous peoples, imposing the early Indo-European language as they went.

Colin Renfrew has proposed a radical rewriting of this scenario. He thinks that a much more gradual spread of language took place as farmers' sons

---

* In some cases richer than ours: the people who spoke this language apparently had at least two words for breaking wind. One of them has come down in various forms: *pardate* in Sanskrit, *perdo* in Greek and *perdzu* in Lithuanian. Remembering Jacob Grimm's rule for changing **p**'s to **f**'s, we get—that's right— "fart."

simply moved up the road to start their own farm as they came of age. And indeed other academics have developed a demographic model that shows that farming could have spread from its origins in the Middle East as far as the British Isles by this sort of passive process, even if the direction each individual took upon leaving the family farm was perfectly random. In other words, you don't have to depend on an eighteen-year-old farmer in 6000 BC hearing the Proto-Indo-European equivalent of "Go west, young man!" It would only require the individuals in each new generation to travel something like eighteen kilometres—in any direction— to keep pace with the spread of agriculture across Europe as it is already known from the archaeological record. But—and Renfrew's opponents see this as a big "but"—for this to work, the original PIE has to be much older than anyone has allowed it to be so far. The farthest back in time most linguists would allow PIE to be is about 4500 BC. Renfrew has to put it back to more than 6000 BC, and he locates the homeland in Turkey, known to archaeologists as Anatolia.

Renfrew hasn't slipped this one through without criticism. Typical are the comments of James Mallory, author of a book on this question called *In Search of the Indo-Europeans*. Dr Mallory argues that if you're going to put these people at any time before 5000 BC, you'll have them in the paradoxical position of speaking a language that has words for wagons, horses, wool, yoke and plough long before there's any tangible archaeological evidence that any of these things existed. Renfrew has been forced not only to defend placing these people much farther back in time, but also to locate them in Turkey, far away from the steppes where most orthodox scholars are happy to put them. He argues that the sort of linguistic evidence that critics like Mallory put forward to prove PIE speakers couldn't have been around in 6000 BC just isn't reliable. He's certain that word borrowing since the original Proto-Indo-European has been common, and is, and always will be, undetected. He argues that innovations, especially in technology, are perfect candidates for borrowing, and of course those would include the words for wagons, yoke and wheel. "Fax" might be an example, which as it spreads from language to language around the world undoubtedly keeps some or all of its original form. Would a linguist three thousand years from now be led to believe that the original word came from Latin or Sanskrit?

Genes come into play here too. In a study published in early 1991, a group of American scientists analyzed blood proteins from people in 3300 different sites across Europe.[27] Proteins are built using blueprints written in the DNA of the genes, and their structure reveals something of their particular gene's structure as well. The study showed that some genes become progressively less common in going from Turkey to northern Europe. This could be explained by the gradual move of farmers westward, as Colin Renfrew has suggested, as long as those farmers interbred with the hunter-gatherers whom they presumably encountered as they went. The more interbreeding, the fewer genes from the original set that would survive.

In addition, the co-creator of the demographic model of gradual advance of farmers, the geneticist Luigi Cavalli-Sforza of Stanford University (whom we will encounter again), has uncovered one startling piece of genetic information about the Basques that is the flip-side of this argument.

The Basques of northern Spain and south-western France have long been a linguistic mystery, because their language is not Indo-European, even though they're completely surrounded by such languages. At one point there was even speculation that Basque had been the language spoken by all before the destruction of the Tower of Babel. It has been described as a stone-age language: the words for tools like pick and axe, even knife, are all based on the root *aitz*, meaning "stone." The speakers of Basque also live right on top of the fabulous caves, like Altamira and Lascaux, that are filled with twenty-thousand-year-old Ice Age art. Basque has a unique grammar, and it's proved very difficult to link it with *any* other language, even though linguists have gone to great lengths to do so. There are parallels, for example, between words in Basque and the Caucasus group, spoken in Asia. In one of those languages, Agul, the word for apple is *zaxar*; in Basque it is *sagar*. The Basque word for rye is *garagar*; in Agul it's *gargar*. But beyond that it's inconclusive. And if you think it's bizarre that a language that's spoken on the shores of the Atlantic Ocean could have connections to the Caucasus mountains, consider that some linguists (in their search for an even more ancient language than PIE) have tried to relate Basque to the Na-Dene languages of North American natives!

Luigi Cavalli-Sforza has shown that Basques have different genes too. He examined the prevalence of the Rh-negative gene, the one that can cause tissue rejection problems in pregnancy if the mother is Rh-negative and the fetus is Rh-positive. The Rh-negative gene shows up in about twenty-five percent of Basques; this is by far the highest percentage in Europe, suggesting that they might represent an ancient European genetic type that resisted being swamped by genes from an advancing wave of Easterners.

So even after a century of research and speculation, there's no agreed-upon home for the Proto-Indo-Europeans. Colin Renfrew pictures farmers spreading out from what is now Turkey, as far back as 6500 BC, and taking their language with them across Europe and Asia. He's going up against a majority view (the one that's in the *Encyclopaedia Britannica*) that places them north of the Black Sea, on the steppes of south Russia and the Ukraine around 4000 BC. In this scenario they were a warlike and highly mobile culture of ranchers and/or shepherds, who from about 4000 BC to 2500 BC engaged in a series of huge migrations, first to Greece, then both east to Asia and west to Europe. They were called the Kurgan people, and they

didn't come peacefully. It is argued that they left
the steppes because of a lack of good grazing land,
and when they reached southern Europe, near the
Danube river, they caused the collapse of the agricultural society that was already there, and
replaced it with herding. And they brought their
language with them.

One of the essential parts of the Kurgan story is
that they domesticated horses, and rode them: they
were mounted warriors. Without the horse it's
hard to see how these migrations of thousands of
kilometres could have taken place. But had they
domesticated the horse? In this case, the language
doesn't help. There *is* a Proto-Indo-European word
for horse: *ekwos*. But if it means domesticated
horses, that would leave no word for wild horse,
which to some experts seems odd. When Colin
Renfrew published his book in 1987 arguing his
slow spread of farming as an alternative to waves
of invading ranchers, he claimed there was no con-
clusive evidence that the people who spoke Proto-
Indo-European had domesticated, let alone ridden,
the horse. He argued—rightly—that the first good
evidence for horses being ridden didn't appear
until about 2000 BC, or even more recently than
that, far too late for the Kurgans to saddle up and
run roughshod over Europe and Asia.

But Dr Renfrew may have been one-upped in
this one. In early 1991 David Anthony, his wife,
Dorcas Brown, and Dimitri Telegin from the
Ukrainian Institute of Archaeology announced
they'd found unequivocal evidence that horses had

been ridden as far back as 4000 BC—two thousand years earlier than any previous evidence suggests.[28] Their most intriguing finding was of the skull of a horse that had apparently been buried in some ritual that involved interring the complete hide, but only the bones from the head, neck and forelegs. However, it's the teeth that are important. The scanning electron microscope reveals wear marks on the teeth that could only have come from a bit, the rope or leather or even metal piece that sits in the horse's mouth and is used to control it. Although the bit is supposed to rest on the gums between the front and back teeth, horses often "chomp at the bit," moving it onto the first set of back teeth. This wears these teeth down, and leaves unmistakable scars and tiny fractures. This six-thousand-year-old horse had been ridden. Its discoverers, and all those who buy the idea of the rampaging hordes spreading Proto-Indo-European across Europe, think this horse has put the ball back in Colin Renfrew's court.

Obviously this story is far from over. And who would want it to be? It's rich in legend, adventure, disagreement and controversy, and there are even hot new discoveries like bit marks on horses' teeth. But the arguments over whether PIE was spread by warlike invaders or peace-loving farmers pale when compared to those which have erupted over the search for the first languages to appear in North America. In this case the only warlike ones are the linguists.

9

<<< Native Tongues

The search for the homeland of the people who spoke Proto-Indo-European is nearly two centuries old, and still most of the important questions have yet to be answered. A lot of talent and energy has been expended in the attempt to reveal who the early Europeans were. In North America we're much newer at this game, but we are playing it just as hard, if not harder. The stakes are the same: analyzing the languages spoken by native North Americans could reveal who they were, and when they came here. And there is a feeling of romance and adventure when the reconstruction of extinct languages promises to bring their speakers to life. In the case of North America, these languages take you back to a time when these words were being uttered by hunter-gatherers living in a world that knew no agriculture, even to a period when long-range mass migrations were bringing people to the Americas *for the first time*. For some, this is going *too* far back.

Why? The reconstruction of Proto-Indo-European is not considered daring or imprudent. Virtually all the experts would agree on a substantial list of words from that ancient language, and they are also comfortable with the idea that it goes back some six thousand years (although Colin Renfrew would like to make it much more ancient than that). So why not use the same techniques and go one step farther back in time, to earlier groups of languages? This is where a lot of those same experts would count themselves out, arguing that to go farther back is impossible: it's okay to jump into the past when you know what you're jumping from. But going back beyond six or even seven thousand years ago raises serious questions in their minds about the accuracy you could *ever* get, let alone the accuracy that some unconventional linguists claim they've already attained.[29]

But as you can imagine, the temptation to jump off into the past where no one else dares to go is overwhelming, and the farther you're willing to leap, the closer you should be getting to an exclusive group of languages, few in number, that covered huge areas of the inhabited world at the time they were spoken. The temptation has been too much for some, and the result has been some fascinating claims, most of which have been met by vicious criticism.

A perfect example is a radical approach taken by a California linguist to understanding the native languages of North America.[30] Where others have collected these into about a hundred and fifty different families, Joseph Greenberg dispenses with these totally, and paints the entire Western Hemisphere in only three linguistic shades: everyone who lived from roughly the lower half of Hudson Bay down to the tip of South America spoke Amerind, with the exception of a small number of peoples in the south-west United States. In the western half of the Northwest Territories, the Yukon and much of Alaska, the dominant language family was Na-Dene, and north of that was Eskimo-Aleut. And that's it. It's probably his lumping together of practically everything into Amerind that has sparked the most controversy. Even non-linguists can get a feeling for how dramatic this gesture is when you realize that of a total of a thousand languages (of which only about six hundred are still being spoken), Na-Dene and Eskimo-Aleut account between them for a mere forty. According to Greenberg, the other nine hundred and sixty can all be traced back to one language: Amerind.

You might think the linguistic world would greet a new Greenberg classification with excitement and even delight, given that his radical classification of African languages (in which he reduced hundreds of language families to four), virtually dismissed when he published it thirty years ago, is now accepted as being correct. That's not quite how his work on native North American languages has been received, unless remarks like, "it should be shouted down" and "misguided and dangerous" are the linguist's version of reluctant praise. His opponents—and everything written about the controversy makes it clear they are not in short supply—think that his technique is sloppy and his conclusions grandiose and exaggerated.[31] At the same time, they are forced to argue that Greenberg's landmark African analysis was somehow easier, or that those languages lent themselves to techniques that the critics now dismiss as sloppy.

Greenberg uses a method called mass comparison: he scans hundreds of different languages looking for words with similar sounds and meanings, especially those which are unlikely to change from generation to generation, or to be borrowed by one language from another. These include words for numbers, pronouns and parts of the body. He argues that words are only borrowed when there's a need to describe something new: "chutzpah" and "macho" have secured themselves a place in English, but the Yiddish and Spanish words for "water" or "head" or "two" haven't. Mass comparison is much more of a "big picture" approach to finding relationships among languages.

In contrast, the standard approach is to compare only a few languages at a time, looking for different sounds that are used in the same way in each, often with the insistence that every step in the conversion of one to the other be demonstrated. Caution characterizes this method—linguists who use it are always wary of words that creep in from other languages or words that change their sounds or meanings with time. Such words can make it appear that two languages share a common ancestral tongue, when they don't. So where Greenberg argues that the letter **n** is used in first-person pronouns and **m** in second-person in hundreds of native North American languages, his opponents are dismissive. They say that **n** and **m** are easy sounds to make (hence the early appearance of the word "mama") and so are likely to be widely used. Greenberg says they're used more in North America, and besides, their very stability makes them good tracers for early languages—they don't change much over time, especially when they are at the beginning of a word. His opponents come back with the claim that he conveniently omits many native languages whose pronouns don't fit this pattern, and includes others where it's impossible to trace this pattern back in time.*

It would be just another in-house academic debate, although a bit nastier than most, except that Greenberg's three ancient families of North American languages are being tied to three waves of migration across the Bering Strait to North America. This adds greatly to the entertainment value by recruiting many more people into the fray; now everyone who's been arguing about who

---

* It's always a bit chancy to describe debates such as this in a book, because the possibility exists that by the time the book is published, the positions will have changed. This is one case where that doesn't seem to be a worry.

first came to North America—and when—can argue about what language they were speaking when they arrived.

For years the accepted date of arrival of the first North Americans has been roughly ten to twelve thousand years ago. These first immigrants were assumed to have crossed the Bering Strait when it was a land bridge (the glaciers of the Ice Age having depleted the oceans of water), then fanned out gradually across North and South America. But this idea is being challenged more and more, and while it's very difficult to dislodge ideas which have had decades to set, a growing number of archaeologists would now accept an arrival date of thirty or thirty-five thousand years ago, and some would go to fifty or even higher. (It is to some extent a matter of opinion because every discovery of a purported camp-site or stone tool has some built-in ambiguity, usually about its age. Within some limits, you believe what you want to believe.)

What does language have to do with this? Joseph Greenberg takes his language map of the Americas to be a history of migrations. Those speaking Amerind came first, eventually spreading throughout the continents, even to the tip of South America. The Na-Dene speakers followed, displacing the Amerinds from the north, and Eskimo-Aleuts came last. Although language reconstruction by itself can't date the arrival of specific groups, Greenberg has had support for a three-wave arrival from research on dental patterns by

Christie Turner II and Stephen Zegura. Independent of Greenberg, they had found specific dental features that seemed to divide North American natives into three groups: Aleuts and Inuit, northwest coast Indians and all the rest. These features can be as simple as the number of roots on the first molar tooth: Asians often have three, while Africans and Europeans usually have only two roots. Turner found three-rooted molars among the teeth from an eleven-thousand-year-old burial in Chile. Differences in roots, shapes of the cutting surfaces, and the number of prominences on molars—more than two dozen differences in all—provide what seems to be clear support for the idea that there were three distinct ancestral groups. Turner and Zegura calculated from the rate of dental change through time that the first of these three groups must have come to North America around fifteen thousand years ago, a date in the traditional ballpark.

When Greenberg first decided that there had been three original language groups in all of the Americas, he assumed that the first, the speakers of Amerind, arrived at what was then the conventional archaeological date of no more than twelve thousand years ago. That was in pretty good agreement with the dental date of fifteen thousand, but it created big problems for him (as his opponents were happy to point out) because in their opinion it wasn't nearly enough time for three original languages to proliferate to the amazing number of native languages in North America today: a thousand languages, classified by most as belonging to a hundred and fifty distinct families. (Greenberg has been quoted as saying that if there are indeed that many distinct language families in North America, there must have been a "prehistoric traffic controller" stationed at the Bering land bridge.) Based on the much better understood case of the Indo-European languages, it would have taken something more like twenty or thirty thousand years, or even more, to get from three to a thousand.

So is Greenberg winning or losing? His attempt to shoehorn three linguistic migrations into the last twelve thousand years has come under heavy fire from linguists, but now, as archaeologists start pushing the date of the first arrival back, they may eventually give him just enough room to hang onto those three migrations.

Is this problem ever going to be resolved? Genetics is playing an important role in this argument, as it has for the origins of the Indo-European languages. The problem is that at the moment, two independent lines of genetic research are heading in opposite directions. Luigi Cavalli-Sforza, the same geneticist who showed that the Basques are unique genetically as well as linguistically, has come up with data suggesting that three different genetic groups can be distinguished in today's native North Americans. By examining structural details of proteins found in the blood, Cavalli-Sforza can infer genetic differences and is able to identify, to his satisfaction, a group corresponding to the Amerind speakers which might still have been together as recently as fifteen thousand years ago. A second genetic group who speak the Na-Dene languages is only distantly related to the Amerinds, and the Eskimo-Aleuts are more distantly related still. Another study backs Greenberg by finding that the genes of three widely separated groups (the Ticuna from South America, the Maya from Central America and the Pima from the United States) share rare genetic patterns. This, plus the fact that the only other place two of these patterns are found is in Asia, is taken by the scientists who did the analysis to mean that these modern Indians are all descended from a single original population which came here over the Bering Strait.

But independent research looking directly at the genetic material itself has not been unanimously supportive. One analysis finds much more genetic diversity than is likely to have arisen from only three different migrations. (The assumption here is that within a single migrating group there would be a lot less genetic variability than there would be between that group and another one coming a thousand years later.) Of course, if there were all kinds of different migrations, it would be hard to hold onto the idea that there was only one original Amerind language with two more to follow.

The only way the Greenbergian idea could be saved from this second set of genetic data is by assuming a single but much older migration. If you can take a deep breath and accept the idea that the first North Americans might have arrived *sixty* thousand years ago—which is pushing it even for the most rabidly anti-establishment archaeologists—then Greenberg lives on. It's really important to keep in mind that all of the genetics is still in the early stages, that none of it is universally accepted, and so whether a particular experiment looks like evidence for or against a theory doesn't yet prove the theory.

Needless to say, even if genetic and/or archaeological evidence were found to be consistent with the idea that there were three major migrations to North America, that doesn't mean that linguists who dispute Joseph Greenberg's methods are going to admit he was right all along. This is a story that will be unfolding—slowly—for some time to come.

There's a tragic irony in the pace of understanding how language came to the Americas. As the linguists fight it out in scholarly journals and at meetings, the very languages they're interested in are dying out.[32] Michael Krauss, a linguist at the University of Alaska, estimates that North American native languages are becoming extinct faster than animals, plants and birds. The problem is simple: most of them are oral languages, and the only people speaking them today are the older generation. When they die, so will the language. Krauss estimates that of close to 200 native North American languages, nearly 150 are no longer being spoken by children.

This isn't only a North American phenomenon: Krauss—and others—estimate that almost half of the world's six thousand languages will be gone in the next hundred years, and nearly half of the three thousand that will be left will eventually go too. They think we will finally be reduced to about five percent of the world's languages that exist today—three hundred in all.

10

The Mother Tongue

"*Tik.*" This could be one of the first words ever spoken on the earth. It means "one" or "pointing finger" or just plain "finger." It might have been spoken in the same sentence as *pal* for "two," or *bur* for "ashes," or even *tali*, meaning tongue. These are the claims of a small but outspoken group of linguistic researchers who believe it's possible to reconstruct the mother tongue, the language they call "proto-World," *the first-ever words spoken on earth.* Most of these linguists have also worked on Nostratic, the Old World equivalent, at least in age, of Amerind. Nostratic is a language supposed to be ancestral to Proto-Indo-European, and is thought by the believers to have been spoken in Europe and Asia some fifteen thousand years ago. That's twice as far into the past as conservative linguists would say it's possible to go. But proto-World would make fifteen thousand years ago look like last week: it is supposed to have been around *a hundred and fifty thousand years ago.*

While "tik" is supposed to have been a word in the first language ever spoken, "ridiculous" is the word that many linguists use to describe that claim. The debate is North America all over again: the older the words that any linguist professes to have identified, the more ludicrous the establishment deems those assertions to be. If in the debate over the origin of native North American languages, Joseph Greenberg is criticized —sometimes with something close to viciousness —for sloppy technique and a tendency to generalize, how do you think the establishment reacts to some researchers' claims that they've recovered as many as a thousand words of Nostratic? Or, as some will say, they've been able to list some of the words from the first language ever spoken? A blend of derision, fury, scorn and dismissal would probably be a good characterization.

From the point of view of popular appeal, it's an unequal argument: it's easy to succumb to the lure of reaching back and making the life of ancient times come alive, whether it is by reliving past lives or reconstructing past languages. In some people's eyes one is as ridiculous as the other, but most of us would like to believe that the past isn't permanently beyond our reach. Why are so many fascinated by Jean Auel's books about the Cro-Magnons and the Neanderthals? Why do the legends of Robin Hood and King Arthur live on? Sure it's true that their struggles are ours today, but part of their appeal must be that they give us a glimpse of humanity in times past. So while you might accept the sense of the arguments that it's really impossible to reconstruct any language older than seven thousand years, your heart wants to believe that *tik*, *bur* and *tali* are the real thing. Rather than dwelling on the yes-it-is, oh-no-it-isn't sort of arguments that characterize this debate, let's just accept that both Nostratic and proto-World are viewed with great suspicion by a large number of linguists, and that it may indeed be true that it will never be possible to reconstruct either, and then go with our hearts; let's leap right past Nostratic and look at what is known, or rather what some daring, even reckless linguists *say* we already know about the world's first language.

Even the believers admit it's a tricky business, because if you are trying to re-create proto-World, your starting materials are languages which themselves have been reconstructed. There's no firm ground to stand on, and you are reduced to comparing lists of words you *think* were part of languages thousands of years old in order to uncover the even more ancient ancestors of *those* words; and none of the words on the lists you're starting with are written anywhere, even in the oldest available stone tablets.

It's also very difficult to demonstrate that you're right: it's one thing to claim that hundreds of native languages are descended from Amerind, because at least there is the possibility of showing that these are more closely related to each other than to the thousands of *other* languages in the world. But when you're claiming that you've found words from the proto-World dictionary, the first words, what do you compare them with? There were, if you are right, no other languages in existence at that time.

Even so, linguists like Merritt Ruhlen in California, Vitaly Shevoroshkin in Michigan, and the Czech Vaclav Blazek have come up with close to two hundred proto-World words.[33] These include terms for body parts, like teeth (*nigi*) and tongue (*tali*), pronouns like I (*ngai*), and even the words *nihwa* and *hwina*, meaning something close to lifeblood. It is going to be difficult to paint a picture of the people who spoke proto-World, as it has been possible—at least partly—to do for the speakers of Proto-Indo-European, simply because the language is so old. A hundred thousand years ago is far too early for farming or domesticating animals (even the fifteen-thousand-year-old Nostratic has no agricultural words, and indeed farming is not supposed to have begun for several thousand years after that). There is very little to go on, but it's likely to have been a life without frills: draw your own conclusions from a language in which (so far) there were words for lice and fleas, but none for emotions.

It might even be a leap of faith to think that language began only once. There could have been several origins, and it would be extremely difficult today, a hundred thousand years after the fact, to tell the difference. This is where genetics, which is playing an increasingly important role in the history of languages, comes back into the picture. The same Luigi Cavalli-Sforza who shows up in the debate over Proto-Indo-European and the native North American languages brings even more important research to the search for proto-World.[34] He and his colleagues have performed detailed genetic studies of aboriginal people around the world, and they find that there is a remarkable parallel between the history of genes and languages.

If you work out the detailed composition of a variety of blood proteins (each of which is the product of a specific gene, but is easier to work with), it's possible to compare the genetic makeup of individuals from many different parts of the world, and from that, calculate how long each unique genetic type has been on its own. The assumption here is that if an original genetically uniform group of people splits up, that uniformity is gradually lost as time passes and people continue to reproduce in isolation from each other: each of the splinter groups will experience their own unique genetic accidents and adopt their own mating patterns. The longer they are apart, the greater the differences in their genes.

A rough analogy would be that after a long relationship (and joint ownership of an old car), you and a friend each bought an identical new car and went your separate ways. The gradual accumulation of unique scrapes and dents, decorations hanging from the rear-view mirror and personalized licence plates would be a measure of the

growing length of time since you had been together. The bumps and scrapes of genetics are mutations, and some of them are perpetuated by
reproduction. And of course, two cars, however
identical they appear at purchase, have their own
idiosyncrasies: so too do any two groups of
humans carved out of a single apparently homoge-
neous population. As the two groups mate only
among themselves, that original genetic variation
will become more apparent.

By measuring the amount of genetic variation
among aboriginal groups, Luigi Cavalli-Sforza
found that Africans were the most different: that
meant that they had long been isolated (genetically) from the rest of humanity. This suggests that
they were the original human stock that gave rise
to all other groups. The genetic distance between
Africans and non-Africans is bigger by far than
that between any other two groups, even those
thought to have been long separated, like Asians
and Europeans. Put it all together and you have a
genetic map of the history of the world's peoples
that shows thousands of years of world-wide
migrations, spreading out originally from Africa.

What's really striking is the comparison
between this genetic map and a chart of relationships among the world's languages; some similari-
ty shouldn't be too surprising in that languages
become separated and diverge with time just as the
people who speak them and their genes do. Even
so the maps' branching points are amazingly simi-

lar, even to the point of suggesting that the controversial and hypothetical ancient languages like Nostratic and an even more all-encompassing group of languages called Eurasiatic have some legitimacy: they can be superimposed on large genetically linked groups of people.

This isn't the only genetic evidence that points to Africa as the original homeland for modern humans. A completely different method first published in 1987 suggested that all of us are descended from one woman (now called "Eve") who lived in Africa a hundred to a hundred and fifty thousand years ago. However, in early 1992 the evidence for Eve took a beating when the original researchers admitted they had used a statistical model incorrectly to reach their conclusions. Even so, many scientists still believe, partly on the basis of the genetic evidence that still stands, and partly on the analysis of fossil bones, that Africa is still the best bet for the homeland of the first modern humans. If true, this would give credence to the idea that the original language might have arisen in the same place at about the same time. At least one researcher has argued that this was no fluke: that it was precisely the possession of language that allowed Africans a hundred thousand years ago to emigrate and take over the world. It would be much more difficult to trace modern languages back to one original mother tongue if the major cultural groups had been split apart for a very long time, especially if there had been several independent origins for modern humans in different parts of the world.*

And if there was a proto-World being spoken way back then, and it was probably somewhere in Africa, is there any way of knowing exactly where?

East of Lake Victoria, near Tanzania and Kenya, all four of the major African language families come close together. This point is right at a boundary between two, just below the southernmost reach of another, and although the vast majority of people who speak Khoisan languages (known as "click" languages because they're full of clicks made by pressing the tongue against the roof of the mouth, teeth or lips and then suddenly releasing air from the lungs) are found much further south, there are two little nearby islands of Khoisan thought to be left over after an original group of Khoisan hunter-gatherers was overrun by farmers speaking other languages.

We'll probably never know whether the four major kinds of African languages had their roots here, let alone whether this might even have been the place where proto-World was first spoken. But in for a dime, in for a dollar, right? Those involved in the search for proto-World are so far out on a

---

* There are those who don't believe this scenario of a single group of Africans migrating out of Africa and around the world, taking already existing groups like Java Man and Peking Man by storm. But these dissenters are, for the moment anyway, in the minority.

linguistic limb already that a little more speculation ("We think the first words were spoken right here ...") isn't going to hurt. And even toying with the idea of a first language brings you inevitably to another hotly debated issue: how did it happen that *Homo sapiens* became the only species on earth (as far as we know) to develop language? To scientists, the answer to that question must involve some evolutionary scenario, and in turn, genetics. If there are genes for language, the search for them promises to be as tricky, and controversial, as the search for the early languages themselves.

11

<<<   Genespeak

The biggest of all the big arguments in language
circles over the last thirty years has been over how
each of us learns to talk: is our language ability
innate, inborn, or do we learn language from
scratch the same way we learn so much of our
other behaviour? Linguist Noam Chomsky, who
claims it's innate, has so dominated this field since
the late fifties that while normally you'd describe a
debate like this as having two sides, his and the
other's, somehow in this case it seems that
Chomsky is at the centre, with all other points of
view swirling around him. Even those who agree
with him that much or all of language ability is
innate still stake out their own slightly different
piece of territory.

Chomsky's view is that the only possible explanation for the ease with which we learn language
and use it (especially given the complexity of the
rules that we employ without even knowing that

we're doing so) is that we are born with special nerve circuits in our brains, the equivalent of a very detailed software package for language. Although he then appears slightly vague about where the language program came from, biologists would step in and argue that the design and construction of such language circuits in the brain, if they exist, would have to be under the direction of a particular set of genes (unless there's something so special about the brain that it can ignore the rules of biology). Would that be one gene, or many? And what would happen if there were mutations in those genes—what sort of linguistic problems might result?

If you don't buy the Chomskian idea that language is innate, you can still allow for the existence of genes important for the development of language, but maintain that they wouldn't necessarily control the ability to talk directly. Instead, they could make possible a range of mental abilities, all of which contribute in some way to language. In other words, genes for smarts, but no genes for language.

Linguist Philip Lieberman of Brown University in Rhode Island has attacked the Chomskian view for years, saying that it is impossible to have a "language organ" in the brain that is identical in everyone, because no genetically determined feature is the same in every individual. A hypothetical language organ would show the same sort of variation from person to person that we see in height, body shape, hair colour or resistance to tooth decay. But, Lieberman continues, any such variation, any weak link in the tightly interconnected set of rules of language would cause the whole thing to fall apart, and that individual would be totally incapable of language. We don't see such individuals, so Chomsky's idea of a language organ is nonsense—it ignores the basic rules of biology.

This argument is, you'll notice, based on what Lieberman says Chomsky says, and Chomsky says that's not what he said. Noam Chomsky doesn't suffer fools gladly, nor is he hesitant to include his colleagues in the definition of "fool." In his final word in an exchange with Lieberman in *The New York Review of Books* in December 1991, Chomsky, after outlining how Lieberman had misunderstood what he (Chomsky) had been saying for years, finished by writing, "Lieberman's other attributions are no less fanciful, and at this level of unseriousness, not worth pursuing."

Lieberman will surely survive these comments (as we'll see in Chapter Thirteen, he can dish it out too), but whether he's right that Chomsky meant what Lieberman said he meant, or not, these two represent the poles of the argument: either language stands alone in the brain, with its own set of genes (Chomsky), or it may have some genes that contribute to it, but it is also dependent on general mental ability (Lieberman).

It's easy to debate the existence of something like language genes as long as none have yet been discovered, but it looks as though that situation has suddenly, and dramatically, changed. Dr Myrna Gopnik is a linguist at McGill University in Montreal, and she has found a group of people who have a genetic language disability.[35] Disability may be too strong a word for some of them, because it's evident that a few who have apparently inherited this problem have learned to work around it. But there's no doubt that their linguistic ability is different, and in one case, Dr Gopnik has been able to trace this problem through three generations in one family.

She stumbled on it several years ago when she was asked to work with a boy named Paul, then eight years old, who talked a mile a minute—fluency was not his problem—but listeners had a hard time understanding what he was trying to say. He would say things like:

"Last time I lost my mommy in the metro. And last time I'm waiting in the [station] and there's another trains coming."

He'd talk about his favourite sport, hockey, and describe how he could watch his favourite team at "the Montreal Forums," even though he knows very well there's only one. Countless other examples in which he was asked to describe scenes in pictures revealed that he had a big problem with plurals. He *knew* there was only one Christmas tree, and many presents under it, but he would say "trees" and "present." He couldn't tell whether the sentences "I can cut a trees" and "I have two puck" sounded right or wrong. And yet he was first in his class in math, so he obviously had no difficulty with numbers themselves. His problem was expressing the difference between singular and plural in language.

Then Dr Gopnik found that it wasn't just plurals he couldn't get right. Words like "he" and "they" also relate to number, and he got them wrong too. If he was asked to repeat, "when it rains," he might say, "when they rain." And even that wasn't all. He also didn't appear to have the automatic system for making the past tense that most of us do. Paul scored zero out of twelve on a test where he was first given a sentence like "Everyday he walks five miles. Yesterday he _____ ?" In this case he answered, "Yesterday he walk." He had obviously figured out ways of compensating for the problem: he often designated the past tense by using the words "last time" at the beginning of the sentence. (Even when he had, probably by luck, used the correct past tense anyway, as in the sentence about the metro above.) After seven years of language training, he still makes these mistakes.

Paul is not alone: there have been reports of other children with the same sorts of problems, including several in Germany and more recently some children in northern Canada who speak Inuktitut. So Paul isn't an isolated case, and English isn't the only language in which this inability to deal with plurals and tenses appears. But it still wasn't clear what was going on, until by chance, Myrna Gopnik stumbled on the discovery that made sense of all this: a family in England, three generations' worth, several of whom had exactly the same problem as Paul. More important, the pattern of who had the problem and who didn't showed that it was caused by a single gene that had been inherited in a perfectly straightforward way.

It's hard to believe: a gene that makes it possible for most of us to be able to add an "s" to a word to make it plural, or choose "they" instead of "he" when it's appropriate, or add "ed" to a verb when it happened in the past! Apparently if you inherit a faulty version of this gene you will never be able to do any of those automatically. Dr Gopnik has come up with some stunning examples of this. In one interview with the grandmother of the English family, Dr Gopnik tested her ability to make plurals of nonsense words (these are used to eliminate the possibility that the person being quizzed might have memorized the correct plurals for real words). One favourite nonsense word used by linguists is "wug," the name given to a little stick figure with a triangular body. Dr Gopnik showed the grandmother one of these, and said, "This is a wug," then pointed to several and asked her to complete the sentence, "These are _____"?

The grandmother paused, then said, "Oh dear, well, carry on ..." When asked again, her response was, "Wugness isn't it? No, no, I see now ... you want me to pair it up ...," and finally, with great difficulty, she came up with "wugs." When faced with another version using "zat," she settled on the plural form "zackle." Others in the English family made one "zat" into many "zacko," and one "zoop" into "zoopez." If she or any of the others had known (unconsciously) the rule for plurals, making "wugs" out of "wug" would have been a cinch. And even when some of the adults did get the right answer, it was obvious they were using a rule they had taught themselves: one woman was overheard saying to herself, "Add an s, add an s." Even at that, she wasn't able to add the "s" in the same way we would. We would change one "mess" into many "messes." She made it into "messs."

Myrna Gopnik suspects that the people with this defective gene have to learn every plural in the English language the same way we learn the unusual ones, like "oxen" and "geese." There's no automatic rule for those—we just memorize them. In fact it's striking how powerful our urge to add "s" can be: my daughter Amelia, as I was writing this, was two months away from her third birthday, and was constantly saying, "I found thems," or "I'm going to get thems." She knew that plurals need an "s." But the people with the defective gene have to memorize "books," "cars" and every other word that we would just automatically add "s" to. And learning one probably doesn't help with any of the others: once they've figured out that the word for more than "book" is "books," they then have to start anew with "car."

There's some additional evidence that their whole notion of number is different from ours. If you're sitting at a table on which are placed a single book and a separate small pile of books, and you're asked, "Point to the book," you're likely to point to the one off by itself. If you're asked to point to the "books," you'll indicate the pile. These people who have some problem with this language gene will point to one in the pile when asked to indicate a "book," and may point to both the single book *and* the pile when asked to point to "books."

As far as Dr Gopnik can tell, these people aren't aware that they have a problem making plurals and past tenses, although they do admit that making conversation is a laborious business. This is borne out by the fact that the family members who have the defective gene speak at a rate of seventy-odd words a minute, while the ones whose gene is normal average more than a hundred and forty. This slower speech might indicate that these people are having to think as they talk, not just about what they want to say, but how to say it: imagine how difficult it would be to have a conversation in which every time you wanted to use the past tense or a plural, you had to remember exactly what to do with that particular word. Speaking deliberately might be the only way you could make your statements reasonably grammatical.

One intriguing footnote to this story has been provided by Elena Plante at the University of Arizona.[36] She has studied the brains of two boys with impaired language (apparently of this sort) and their parents, and she's found that one part of the brain in these people is unusually *large*: it's the part of the brain that corresponds to Wernicke's area, the area up and behind the ear on the left side of the brain, damage to which often leaves the person capable of fluent but nonsensical speech. But there's one important difference in this case: it's that part of the brain all right, but on the *right* side, not the left. What does this mean? The right side usually has very limited language abilities, and besides, in this case it's not damaged, it's *bigger*. At the same time, the corresponding area on the left, Wernicke's area, appears completely normal. And a gene causes this difference? There's a glimpse of something really fascinating here, but nobody has a clue what it is—yet.

This discovery of a gene that is apparently responsible for the rules governing past tenses and plurals has a lot to say about the connection between genes and language. First, it makes it much more difficult to argue that language is simply a byproduct of learning, or that there are no genes directly responsible for it. It seems there are. It also eliminates the possibility that there is a single language gene, because although these people have apparently incurable problems with verb tenses and plurals, they have no problem with word order or complicated sentence structures. This suggests that there might be several different brain systems for language that work together—whether they were put together one by one over time, or all at once, can't be answered yet.

In a way, this family which carries a defective language gene gives us a glimpse of how we all might deal with language. Remember that it appears as if they are forced to memorize every plural, and every past tense, as if it were an irregular. All of us have to learn that the past tense of "buy" is "bought." They have to learn the past tense of any verb the same way: they can't automatically derive "turned" from "turn," as we seem to be able to. Dr Steven Pinker, a linguist at the Massachusetts Institute of Technology, has suggested that this is a picture of the way our brains are organized to learn language.[37] Some of it, as Noam Chomsky has long argued, is inborn: that would include rules like changing present to past tense, or singular to plural, and these rules would apply to all the so-called regular nouns and verbs. The rest of the nouns and verbs are irregular, and we have to learn them case by case. Pinker's convinced that adding "ed" to a verb is an innate rule that applies not only to all kinds of verbs in common use, but also to new ones: "He faxed it to me." One of the most striking examples he uses to back up this idea is his demonstration that whenever we encounter verbs that we intuitively perceive as having been derived from nouns, we automatically form the past tense by adding "ed," even if the word contains an irregular verb! So, for instance, a showoff is said to have "grandstanded," not "grandstood." He "flied out" to end the inning, not "flew out." And the penalized player "highsticked," not "highstuck" the other guy. Steven Pinker says we use these past tenses because these novel verbs are stored in our brains as nouns, and nouns can't have past tenses, so we simply apply the automatic rule of "ed" to them when we form the past tense.

The family that Myrna Gopnik has studied would presumably not make these automatic decisions about past tense, because they don't have the whatever-it-takes to apply the automatic rule. What that single missing gene actually does is anybody's guess: it's a very long way from identifying the specific protein that a gene makes (and that *is* what genes do) to deciding how that single protein can eliminate a grammatical rule in the brain! About the only thing that can be said is that however farfetched the idea of a gene, or protein, for grammar sounds, there are precedents for a single gene having far-ranging, even weird effects: children who have a kind of retardation called Williams syndrome are nonetheless very good at language, and in fact when asked to name animals will come up with "unicorn," "aardvark" or "ibex," instead of the normal "dog," "pig" or "cat." The gene that causes this condition plays a role in the processing of calcium in the brain. That just shows how difficult it might be to "explain" how one gene in a family leaves them unable to make plurals or past tenses.

At the same time, the existence of this gene suggests there could be others. They haven't been identified yet, but could we be hearing the subtle evidence of some as yet undiscovered genetic language deficits in daily conversation? We all know people who are better or worse at language, ranging from some who seem to be able to spin long, complex but beautifully assembled sentences one after the other, to those who are terse and straightforward; some who never get to the point, others who never embellish. If people with a relatively severe genetic disability like the inability to make plurals and past tenses can figure out ways of getting by, so too might many others who are less severely compromised. But proving such people exist would be pretty difficult: if they're employing some unconscious strategy to overcome a genetic language problem, and it's working, how would they ever be found out?

12

<<< Now You're Talking!

How humans began to talk, and when, are questions that will almost certainly never be answered. There are just too many pieces of this puzzle that had to be in place at the right time, and most of these, as far as anyone knows, have left no trace. Speech requires the possession of the right kind of vocal machinery and an auditory system specifically tuned to human speech, the brain power to run both of those, and, in addition, plenty of brain cells to tie those two together and link the whole system to the thinking brain.*

---

* Another problem is explaining how words (most of which have nothing to do with what they stand for) were created. There have been at least four theories that seek to explain how spoken language might have developed from sounds early humans were already making: the *bow-wow* theory argues that onomato-

Of course, knowing that it's probably impossible to answer these questions hasn't stopped scientists from trying, and some very entertaining speculation has come out of it. It's important to remember, though, that in trying to answer the questions how and when we started talking, just as in the search for the first languages, it's all claims and counter-claims—fascinating ideas but not necessarily statements of truth.

One way of trying to figure out when talk began is to study the fossil skulls of ancient hominids, those creatures thought to be our distant ancestors. Although bones are all we have left of them, if there is enough of the skull left, it is sometimes possible to get a glimpse of what the brain inside was like. As the brain grows in the fetus and young child, it presses against the inside of the skull, leaving faint markings in the bone. The most prominent of these are left by the blood vessels at the brain's surface, but it's even possible to get an idea of the general shape and size of the brain, and

---

poeic words, like bow-wow, whoosh and tweet-tweet could have evolved into words, and that fairly limited vocabulary would eventually be joined by others that didn't mimic what they were describing. The *pooh-pooh* theory says (seriously!) that interjections, like "hmmmph" and "bah" would become the first words. The *yo-he-ho* theory is based on the guess that ritualized chanted sounds became language, and the *la-la* theory sees words coming from children's singing.

where the most prominent bulges were.

Occasionally, long after the actual brain tissue had decayed away, fossil skulls were filled with sediment that gradually hardened and pressed against the inside of the skull much as the brain had. That hardened sedimentary "brain" will then have on it some of the markings of the original. It's also possible to make a cast of the inside of an empty skull by pouring latex into it. These casts of ancient brains—natural or poured—have shown that there was a steady increase in the size of the brain from the Australopithecines, which predate any members of our genus *Homo*, through all our early ancestors finally to modern humans, *Homo sapiens*. (See Chapter Thirteen for the Neanderthals.)

Brain size doesn't necessarily tell us anything about language. But there are at least two skulls of *Homo habilis*, "man the toolmaker," that show much more. *Homo habilis*, although on the way to becoming human, was still very far removed from modern people, with a brain only about half the size of ours. This species died out a little more than 1,500,000 years ago, and yet the casts of two *habilis* skulls, one from Kenya, the other from Olduvai Gorge (the human fossil site made famous by Louis Leakey), have well-developed Broca's and Wernicke's areas on the left sides of their brains. Of course we can never know what they were doing with this brain tissue, and there's really no evidence of any sort that would suggest *Homo habilis* was a good conversationalist. But, if you believe the faint impressions on the inside of these skulls (and not everyone who's looked at them does), then you can at least assume that our ancestors more than a million years ago were neurologically and anatomically ready for speech, even if they didn't actually use it.

What is different about a brain that's ready for speech? This brings us right into the arguments over *how* language started, and you can get an insight into this by remembering everything you can of your high-school English: grammar, sentence structure, even tenses of verbs. At the time, these details probably seemed pretty tiresome, but think of them not as rules to be memorized but as the nuts and bolts of English. They ensure that thoughts and words are organized logically so that you end up with a sentence or a speech that makes sense.

Talk isn't the only thing we do that needs to be organized and logical: driving a car, planning your shopping route through the supermarket, even plotting and executing strategy in a game need some sort of organization and planning—the equivalent of grammar and sentence structure—before they'll work. Based on the idea that a brain that can do any of these things should be able to do all of them, experts have for decades been arguing that there should be some way of detecting when our ancestors had acquired the sort of reasoning capabilities that would have made language possible, even though they wouldn't have been writing down what they were saying (everyone

agrees that writing came long after talking began).
Our ancestors who could speak were also engaged
in other complicated—and in some ways analo-
gous—activities, some of which must surely have
left traces behind. Making stone tools is a perfect
example.

Tool-making seems a long way from talking, but
those who have studied both have argued that in
crucial ways they are very much alike. The earliest
tools are more than two million years old, and they
are pretty simple: just a chunk of rock with a couple of pieces knocked out of the sides to make a
sharp edge. But as the few twentieth-century
humans who have taught themselves how to make
identical stone tools have found, even the first
tool-makers knew exactly what they were doing.

These tools called bifacial choppers reveal that
their makers, while perhaps not having the greatest
finesse, had learned to follow a simple sequence
of actions. The bifacial chopper is a round stone
that fits into your hand and has had two or three
pieces knocked off opposite sides to make a cutting edge. These pieces have to be taken off in the
proper order, and oriented with some overlap so
that a sharp edge results.

But there's more to it than just following a single set of hand movements. In some cases the individuals that made these tools appear to have
travelled several kilometres away from their main
camp-site to get good stones. As well, some stones
in a riverbed have hairline fractures on their surface, and usually these will also have internal

flaws that cause them to flake unpredictably. The tool-makers must have recognized these as bad material, because the kind of fragments that result when these stones are flaked are hardly ever found in the remains of tool kits.

All of this suggests a lot of planning and thinking through a sequence of future events, the same sort of mental activities, it's argued, that are needed for making up sentences. (After all, it's almost always true that the first few words of a sentence reveal that the subsequent words have already been planned and assembled.) This is not a case of arguing that ancient people needed language to be able to make stone tools; it wasn't necessarily so difficult that the tool-maker had to have someone looking on and saying, "Now, knock that flake off ... no, no, you're taking too much ... just ease back there and knock a *small* flake off ..." Instead, the speculation is that tool-making and talking require the same ability to plan several steps into the future, to know that you have to knock off the first flake of stone before you can go ahead to the second, and to have in your mind the completed thought, whether that's a paragraph or a spearhead, before you've even begun. And even in this *Homo habilis* tool kit, the most primitive of them all, there is another hint that the brain, even at this primitive stage, was moving towards language.

As I mentioned above, the so-called bifacial chopper, a rock with pieces struck off opposite sides, is one of the commonest tools found from one and a half to two million years ago. There is also a "unifacial" chopper, in which the basic stone is simply struck, then rotated slightly in the hand, struck again, and so on. The chips or flakes that come off have a different shape depending on which hand was holding and rotating the target stone, and which held the striking stone, the hammer. Nicholas Toth at Indiana University has found that the leftovers at the ancient camp-sites suggest that most of the tool-making had been done by right-handers, those holding the hammer or striking stone in the right hand.[38] This opens the door to some interesting speculation: the right hand is controlled by the left side of the brain. Today, most right-handers have their primary language centres on the same side, the left. To find that tool-makers more than a million and a half years ago already had brains with some right-left specialization raises the question as to whether those brains were already developing language centres. Indeed some scientists have already suggested that there was a connection in ancient humans between the evolving manipulative skill of the right hand, and the potential for talk.

Curiously enough, there is evidence from stroke patients suggesting a connection between hand movements and language. Dr Doreen Kimura at the University of Western Ontario has found that damage close to Wernicke's area, the language centre at the back on the left side of the brain, is often associated with difficulty in moving *both* left and right hands.[39] (People with Wernicke's aphasia have no trouble producing fluent speech, but it's filled with nonsense words and leads off in unexpected directions.) Many of these same patients have difficulty when asked to salute, wave, or make the motions of using a hammer or scissors (without actually having them in hand). They will hesitate, or repeat part of the motion several times, or move clumsily. They have particular trouble moving from one hand position to the next in the sequence, but have no trouble repeating the same movement over and over once they've achieved it.

Dr Kimura points to the parallel with speech: people with Wernicke's aphasia can say the same syllable like **ba**, over and over, but are much slower and make mistakes if they're supposed to say **ba-ga-da**: the disabilities in speech and movement are similar. She has speculated that the fact that the left side of the brain controls sequences of hand movements may be the result of our ancient ancestors coming to depend on the right hand for the fine work in making stone tools. If the first languages used gestures rather than sounds, then it would be natural that sequences of gestures would come under the control of the same brain centres as hand movements. Then you already have the left side of the brain dealing with a kind of language—it's a relatively short step from controlling sequences of movements that convey ideas to sounds that do the same.

More recently the California linguist Patricia Greenfield has claimed a connection between the progress children make in developing strategies for tasks—like nesting different-sized cups one inside the other—and their ability to use more and more complicated language.[40] She suggests that a single brain area on the left is at first responsible for both, but then splits into two regions specialized for manual and verbal abilities. Greenfield sees no reason why the same sort of split couldn't have been one of the crucial events in our evolution which allowed speech to appear.

The evidence provided by the brains and tools of *Homo habilis* can at best be taken as hints that these ancestors had brains that were shaping up for speech. No one seriously thinks they talked: the genetic and linguistic arguments for the first language can be taken back *at most* 150,000 years. So anything happening ten times farther back— 1,500,000 years—can only be setting the scene. Of course a primitive version of sign language could have appeared early, and developed slowly as our ancestors evolved. But the question of when *talk* actually started cannot be answered by looking at ancient tool kits: the primitive tools of *Homo habilis* stayed unchanged for 1,500,000 years, an unimpressive record of dynamism and innovation. You have to wait an enormous length of time— right up to about 30,000 years ago—before you see the development of something that many specialists think is the true indicator that people are finally talking: art.

The beautiful cave paintings at Lascaux and Altamira, the so-called "Venus" figurines, and decorated spear-throwers and harpoon heads are all less than thirty thousand years old. These were made by physically modern people, *Homo sapiens*. And while stone tools are simply instruments of survival, paintings and carvings go far beyond: it's obvious from images like that of a crouching figure wearing reindeer antlers, the exaggerated breasts and buttocks of figurines and even the way paintings were arranged on cave walls and ceilings that the artists were doing something more than just cataloguing the animals and people of the time. There's also evidence that the recipes for colours must have been passed down through dozens of generations. It's hard to imagine all of this happening without language. But in one way this seems much too late; the explosion of art takes place more than seventy thousand years after the appearance of fully modern human beings, with brains the size and shape of ours. These are, according to a popularized scientific version of the story, the people that came out of Africa and swept over the earth. Some wonder if one of the reasons they could have done that was because they were good talkers. But why they would then wait so long before starting to paint on cave walls is an unanswered question.*

Everything I've described so far supports the idea that language could only develop after the brain had been pre-adapted for it, possibly by developing skills in manoeuvring the right hand that later made enunciation and rapid-fire speech

---

* A lack of corporate sponsors?

possible. But there are some, including the foremost language researcher of this century (if not of all time), Noam Chomsky, who have claimed that language was much more sudden in its appearance and was distinct in its capabilities from all other mental capacity. Chomsky believes that humans have a unique language organ in the brain which contains a set of rules that dictates how every one of the five or six thousand languages on earth is to be spoken. He has suggested from time to time that something sudden and extraordinary must have happened to the human brain to produce that language organ. He even has gone so far as to suggest that the normal mechanisms of evolution may not apply to something like the brain that contains billions of neurons in a relatively small space. But outside of admitting that there are surely things about life we haven't yet imagined, it's pretty difficult to see how the brain could have developed language in some as yet unimaginable but practically miraculous way.

Outside of a miracle, the only truly sudden event that can happen to a species is a mutation in a gene, a change that's almost always disadvantageous, but can sometimes confer some sort of advantage on the animal possessing it. But could an alteration of a single gene have produced something as complex as language?

Most of the key factors would already have to have been in place: the ability to make the whole range of speech sounds, an auditory system to decode them, and a brain to connect thoughts with sounds and eventually words and sentences. And, as some have suggested, maybe there already was the equivalent of a dictionary (sounds and/or gestures that stood for things) and a separate ability to put actions and ideas in the right order, and some genetic lightning bolt brought those two together, making it possible to create meaningful sequences of words.

But in evolutionary terms this would be the appearance of the capacity for language *overnight*, and in a single individual. Mutations don't appear simultaneously in groups or communities. Doesn't this create the awkward scenario of one person born with the novel ability to string together sentences with clauses in them, with no one to impress? It sounds like the picture-phone, the kind where you can see the person you're talking to. If you are the first person to buy one, who do you talk to? There is a counter-argument: you would likely pass the gene on to some of your offspring, and then at least within your (ever-growing) family, communication would become more sophisticated. But the idea that there was a single, abrupt change from some sort of pre-language to the full-fledged item seems a little hard to believe.

That leaves the more traditional evolutionary approach, which would argue that there are several genes for language (see Chapter Eleven for a good candidate for one of them), and they each evolved, perhaps independently, or possibly in concert, to their present state. For this to have happened, every change, every mutation in any one of those genes would have to have been beneficial to the person in whom it occurred, otherwise those changes wouldn't have been passed on to future generations.

But how much of an advantage would there be as the result of a slight change in the ability to communicate? The old argument that Creationists like to use against evolution comes up again here in a slightly different form: "What good is five percent of an eye?" or in this case, "What good is half a rule for extracting noun phrases from embedded clauses?" Defenders of the idea that language could have evolved step by step argue that five percent vision is clearly better than none at all, and variations of a language that are much less sophisticated than the language itself, like the talk used by toddlers, immigrants, tourists, headlines and telegrams are much better than no language at all.

A man who became best known for his work trying to teach language to apes, David Premack, has taken another tack in wondering about the value of ever-more sophisticated language ability to our ancient ancestors. He asks if it would have been a great advantage for one of them to say, "Beware of the short beast whose front hoof Bob cracked when, having forgotten his own spear back at camp, he got in a glancing blow with the dull spear he borrowed from Jack."[41] Maybe it would, maybe it wouldn't, and maybe an elaborate sentence like that is beside the point. Wouldn't it have been advantageous to be able to express the difference between, "The sabre-tooth tiger is on the other side of the hill," and "The sabre-tooth tiger is on *this side* of the hill"? Or the difference between these two (whispered) remarks: "Throw your spear after I charge," and "Throw your spear when I charge"?

The evolution of language is harder to study than the evolution of humans or any other living things. There are no fossil bones, no vestigial organs, and no relict species (like the cockroach or the lungfish): all modern languages are equally complex.* There is only the evidence that language comes from our brains, the assumption that our brains have been shaped by evolution, and the fact that there must have have been a time when our ancestors—and their brains—didn't have language. But how did it get there? We can only guess.

---

* But see Derek Bickerton's ideas in Chapter Eighteen.

13

<<< The Neanderthals, or
Can Pigs Talk?

In William Golding's *The Inheritors*, published in
the mid 1950s, a small band of primitive Neanderthal people encounters a group of Cro-Magnons
(physically modern people), and one by one they
are kidnapped, killed or left to die. These Neanderthals are to be pitied: a gentle people so close to
the earth that they believe they have come from it,
who communicate by a blend of shared mental
"pictures" and words. For most of them, those
words don't come easily, and their names reflect
the simplicity of their thoughts: Lok, Liku, Fa.
They are no match for the more sophisticated, bet-
ter-armed Cro-Magnons whose language is as elaborate as their spirituality and their art.

Jean Auel's long-running and best-selling series
about life in Europe at the time of the Neanderthals and the Cro-Magnons began with *The Clan of
the Cave Bear*, published in 1980. Her Neanderthals are a lusty grinning bunch with a strong mag-

ical bent who communicate more by gestures and movements (and by a kind of intuition similar to Golding's shared pictures) than words. They have trouble with abstract concepts, and even more trouble getting their tongues around the words that Ayla, the Cro-Magnon they adopted, can utter.

In the same year as Jean Auel's *The Clan of the Cave Bear*, a much less well known book called *Dance of the Tiger* was published by palaeontologist Björn Kurtén. In an unusual move for a scientist, Kurtén translated his scholarly knowledge of life in the Ice Age into a novel. His plot was similar to Auel's except that a Cro-Magnon *boy* is adopted by Neanderthals. Kurtén's Neanderthals were also different linguistically from their Cro-Magnon rivals. Their speech was deliberate, and relied heavily on the pitch of their spoken sounds, mostly because they were limited to only two vowel sounds, **ah** and **oh**.

All three books portray the Cro-Magnons as more sophisticated verbally than the Neanderthals, and by implication better equipped to survive. They are all exploring the question that has haunted fossil hunters for a hundred years. Why did the Neanderthals, who lived successfully in Europe for nearly 100,000 years, die out suddenly 35,000 years ago, at almost exactly the same time that Cro-Magnons arrived in Europe. Did the two species fight to the death? Did modern humans simply outcompete the Neanderthals for the available resources? Were these modern people smarter? But of these three authors, only Björn Kurtén specified a Neanderthal language deficit—the inability to speak any vowels other than **ah** and **oh**—that scientists have actually suggested might have been their downfall. A vowel shortage is the basis of a hotly disputed theory about why the Neanderthal people were eventually wiped off the face of the earth. It's a theory that attributes the ultimate triumph of the Cro-Magnons (modern people) not to their superior brains but to their throats.*

The Neanderthals are a handy target for those searching for a clever metaphor for low-browed

---

* Fossil people are generally named after the place they were found: Java Man, Peking Man and so on. The first Neanderthal was found in the Neander valley in Germany, although it's now known they lived all across Europe into the Middle East, from about 130,000 to 35,000 years ago. They are technically called *Homo sapiens neanderthalensis*; they are a subspecies of modern humans. The people who apparently arrived in Europe about 35,000 years ago used to be called Cro-Magnons, because that's the place in France where the first fossil was found. Now fossils of that type of human have been found in southern Africa and the Middle East, and in those areas they go back much farther than in Europe: to about 100,000 years ago. So they are officially known today as "physically modern people" and their scientific name is *Homo sapiens sapiens*: that's what we are. There are some scientists who argue that the two subspecies interbred, but at the moment that is a minority opinion.

stupidity. I had no trouble collecting several references to Neanderthals in newspapers and magazines a couple of years ago: "near neanderthal TV cop Ric Hunter ...," "British soccer hooliganism ... rumbles tattooed hairy and neanderthal ...," and then-trade minister John Crosbie vowing to achieve a free-trade deal with the United States despite the "neanderthals" opposed to it.

Those who write and speak this way are about forty years out of date, stuck in a time when Neanderthals were seen as shuffling, bent-over, semi-intelligent pre-humans, the archetypal cavemen. Alley Oop without the dinosaurs. This image did originally have some scientific backing. The first detailed examination of a Neanderthal skeleton was in 1912, by the French scientist Marcellin Boule. Using the bones found in 1908 at the archaeological site called La Chapelle-aux-Saints, Boule re-created what he thought this individual would have looked like when he lived, sixty thousand years ago, and came up with a short, bent-over, heavily muscled man. His head, marked by heavy brow ridges and a sharply receding forehead, jutted forward from the body. And that's the way Neanderthals were protrayed for the next fifty years in science, and still today in popular culture.

Boule was right about some things, but very wrong in others. The Neanderthals *did* have heavy brow ridges and low foreheads, but their brains were bigger, on average, than our brains today. Exactly what this means is unclear: although in general a bigger brain signals greater intelligence, when you're talking about a difference of 100 cubic centimetres of a total of 1400, as you are here, it's not at all certain that the extra 100 means more smarts. (One hundred cubic centimetres is about four ounces—a small glass of wine.) Some of the greater volume of the Neanderthal brain is at the back in a part of the brain called the cerebellum, which is primarily responsible for the coordination of movement. Given that these people were much more heavily muscled than we are (you can tell that by thickness of the bones and the large anchoring points for muscles), and that there's evidence from bone wear that they moved in irregular ways (broken-field runners rather than purposeful striders), it's possible that the extra brain tissue was controlling movements, not thoughts.*

But the image of Neanderthals as shuffling, stooped and awkward people, as depicted by Boule in 1912, is completely wrong. He didn't realize that the La Chapelle-aux-Saints individual had had severe arthritis, and his bones were deformed as a result. So while Boule might have been correct to suspect that this individual was bent over, that

---

* However, recent imaging experiments have shown that the cerebellum responds when a person performs the linguistic task of changing nouns to verbs, and even the most experienced cerebellar specialists acknowledge that exactly what this part of the brain does—and it amounts to about ten percent of the total brain volume—is still in good part unknown.

was not the typical Neanderthal posture. They were shorter than modern people, and much more heavily built, but they stood as erect as we do. They were not ape-like from that point of view, nor did they have simian faces. An expert on Neanderthals once described the face to me as what you'd have if someone took your cheekbones and nose and pulled them forward: a protruding face with a very prominent nose.

But was it stupidity that eliminated them? After all, having lived in Europe and the Near East for nearly one hundred thousand years, they appear to die out suddenly upon the arrival of humans like us. It's impossible to be precise about how rapidly they became extinct, but most experts would agree it didn't take much more than a couple of thousand years. And most theories about their demise have pointed to lesser intelligence as their downfall—that they simply weren't able to compete with people who had modern brains, and were therefore highly intelligent. What evidence there is tends to support the idea that indeed they might not have had what it took. Their stone tools are relatively crude, and more important, they created no works of art: no paintings on cave walls, no figurines, nothing of any kind, let alone of the breathtaking style and variety that their successors left behind. On the other hand, they could have been accomplished weavers, great wood carvers, even first-rate tattooers, and we'd never know it, because none of those materials are preserved in the fossil record.

But there's more bad news: in some of the latest analyses of Neanderthal camp-sites at Combe Grenal in France, veteran American anthropologist Lewis Binford claims that he finds no evidence that the people who lived there planned ahead. For instance, there are annual runs of salmon in a nearby river, runs that would have provided an incredible windfall for the locals, but there's no sign that they took hundreds of fish at a time, stored them and ate them later. Binford argues that's the case wherever the remains of Neanderthals are found—there's never any evidence of planning for the future.

There is an exception to this rule: a Neanderthal burial ground in Iraq excavated in the 1950s appeared to provide evidence that Neanderthals did think about the far future—the time after death. In a cave called Shanidar, a Neanderthal man was found buried amidst the pollen from several different species of flowers, some of which had apparently been brought into the cave, since there was no evidence that they actually grew just outside. There were even suggestions that there was careful thought guiding the particular selection of flowers, because they would bloom at different times of the year. Did the find at Shanidar mean that the brutish Neanderthals thought about life after death? There were other skeletons too, in other caves, one in particular surrounded by a circle of goat horns. But recently doubts have been cast even on these discoveries: maybe the pollen blew in, or was carried in by rodents; perhaps the goat horns were there because several goat carcasses had been left in that cave. Maybe the fetal positions of the dead were just natural after-death postures, and didn't signify even a plain burial. On the other hand, there is (so far) undisputed evidence that they must have taken care of their sick and lame. That individual from La Chapelle-aux-Saints studied at the beginning of this century had had severe arthritis for years before he died: there's no way he could have taken care of himself in a hunter-gatherer society. One of Jean Auel's principal characters in *The Clan of the Cave Bear*, the Mog-ur, was based on a real skeleton, the skull of which was severely damaged on the left side, resulting in a deformed right leg (surprisingly, Auel did not portray this medicine man as having any language difficulty, even though his language hemisphere was badly damaged).

At best most of the evidence *for* Neanderthal intelligence is equivocal or disputed, and when added to the absence of art and advanced tools, and the symbolic thinking that goes with them, it's possible to argue that a lack of smarts did in the Neanderthals. They survived in the extremely harsh environment of Ice Age Europe for ninety thousand years, but couldn't deal with competition.

This is where physically modern people, the Cro-Magnons, come in. The Neanderthals might never have died out if they had not had competition. But it looks like push came to shove 35,000 years ago, and when it did, the Neanderthals were out and the Cro-Magnons were in.*

Some researchers think language was what separated the two. In both *The Inheritors*, and *The Clan of the Cave Bear*, the Neanderthals are not yet completely verbal: they use mental pictures or their hands to supplement what they cannot yet say. In Björn Kurtén's *Dance of the Tiger* the Neanderthals' speech is incomplete, because they can't make the vowel sounds **aw**, **ee** and **oo** (as in hot, heat and hoot). This seemingly slight impediment is the basis for one scientific explanation of why the Neanderthals died out.

This theory was first suggested more than twenty years ago by linguist Philip Lieberman and anatomist Edmund Crelin.[42] They didn't bother looking at casts of the inside of Neanderthal skulls (that information can't really give you a firm yes or no anyway). Instead they asked the question: what speech sounds could the Neanderthals have made? From a reconstructed Neanderthal skeleton

---

* This used to be a neat picture. The primitive form of human is already there, the modern form comes in, wipes them out and that's that. But in the 1980s, skeletons discovered in Israel made this picture a lot more confusing. It seems as if, at least in the Middle East, Neanderthals and modern people were living together (or at least in each other's neighbourhood) for 60,000 years! Why could they co-exist for so long, only to have the scales suddenly tipped in Europe 35,000 years ago? This new puzzle has compounded the mystery of why the Neanderthals died out.

(the celebrated La Chapelle-aux-Saints bones) they inferred what the size and shape of the space between the lips and the top of the larynx must have been. This of course is the space which—by its layout in modern humans—makes possible the individual vowel sounds. Lieberman and Crelin concluded that Neanderthals were like chimpanzees and modern human infants, insofar as the space inside their throats and mouths went. The main difference between all these and modern adults is that in adults, there's a sharp turn at the back of the throat. The straight line in from your teeth ends abruptly at the back of your throat, and you have to turn ninety degrees downwards to the voice-box. In chimps, babies and—these researchers argued—Neanderthals, the path from lips to voice-box was a gentle curve. No abrupt turns. This creates a completely different acoustic chamber, and as computer models seem to show, one that doesn't permit the creation of some vowels: vowels like **oo**, **ee** and **aw** that neither chimps or infants are able to make either. (The theorists also claim that the Neanderthals would have had trouble with consonants like **g** and **k**.)

Lieberman's and Crelin's model of the Neanderthal vocal tract differs in many ways from ours. Because it has a gradual bend rather than a right turn, the larynx sits high in the neck, and can be connected directly to the airspace at the back of the nose. An animal with this arrangement could have air from the nose flow directly to the lungs, bypassing the mouth, and so could breathe and drink at the same time. The Neanderthals were that way, chimpanzees are that way, and modern humans begin life that way. This allows infants to breathe through their noses and nurse at the same time. However, in humans the larynx migrates downwards from this original high position, ending in its adult position at about the age of eighteen months, conferring on infants of that age an expanded repertoire of speech sounds, but at the same time creating a space above the larynx large enough that food can detour into the larynx from the food tube and get stuck, sometimes with fatal consequences. That disadvantage, according to this theory, is outweighed by having the potential to make more and better speech sounds. This theory would suggest that Neanderthals never choked to death on their food, and that had the Neanderthals prevailed over the Cro-Magnons, we would never have needed Henry Heimlich and his manoeuvre!

Lieberman and Crelin further argue that there would have been dramatic differences between the tongues of modern humans and the Neanderthals. Our tongue not only lies on the floor of the mouth but also extends back down the throat, forming the front wall of the space behind the mouth called the pharynx. That particular configuration allows the tongue to alter the sound qualities of that space dramatically by changing shape and position. The Neanderthal's tongue was confined to the mouth (for it to have extended down the throat it would have had to be as long as an ape's tongue) and this all-in-the-mouth tongue had much more restricted sound-altering abilities.

This might sound like a lot of fuss to be making over three vowels, but the sounds **aw**, **ee** and **oo** are known to be easily perceived, and are an important part of most world languages. Lieberman and Crelin have never argued that the lack of these sounds meant that the Neanderthals couldn't speak, but it would, they think, have made their speech slightly less intelligible, slightly more prone to error, and slower. If they were in competition for the somewhat scanty resources of Ice Age Europe with people who had modern larynxes and so could make the entire range of modern speech sounds, that slightly poorer speech might have been their undoing. Lieberman himself has made different estimates of how much less efficient the Neaderthals' speech might have been, from five percent to thirty percent, but the exact percentage isn't really crucial to the argument.

Naturally this idea has not been accepted by all—is there any idea in language research that is? From the beginning, Lieberman and Crelin were criticized, especially for using the La Chapelle-aux-Saints skull to make their measurements and computer models. The critics argued that the arthritis that had crippled this man might also have altered his jaw and the bottom of his skull enough to make any judgment about vocal tracts inapplicable to Neanderthals in general. Others claimed that the way Crelin and Lieberman had put together the pieces of the jaw and throat, Neanderthals would have had much more serious problems to contend with than simple speech impediments—they wouldn't have been able to swallow! But none of the criticisms have killed the theory, and while it's still controversial after twenty years, it's also still with us, and in fact is enjoying some revived interest, thanks to an unusual fossil find in Israel.[43]

In the late 1980s, researchers digging at the burial site at Kebara in Israel found something that had never been found before in association with any Neanderthal bones. A hyoid bone. This is a U-shaped bone that sits under the back of the tongue, right at the level of the chin. It isn't attached to any other bones, being held in place instead by attachments to muscles and ligaments in the area. The crucial thing about this bone is that it is like a modern human hyoid—there's nothing primitive or unusual about it. Nor is there anything odd about the positions and sizes of muscles that were attached to it (as attested to by the marks they left on the bone). The discoverers have therefore suggested that if a Neanderthal's hyoid bone is just like a modern human's, then it can be assumed that the other parts of the vocal apparatus, especially the position of the larynx, could easily have been modern too. That being the case, the Neanderthals could have been as well-spoken as we are. In particular, this hyoid bone is nothing like a chimp's hyoid, even though Lieberman and Crelin and their colleagues have always said the two should be similar.

This discovery, or rather the claims being made

about it, have not pleased Philip Lieberman. Never a man to take criticism casually (he uses words like "irrelevant," "misses the point" and "dubious" when discussing those skeptical of his ideas), he has argued that using the criteria the Israeli discoverers used, one could argue that the pig hyoid is human-like, and that therefore "we could assert with equal confidence that pigs can talk." Baruch Arensburg, one of the discovers of the hyoid bone, didn't appear to be shaken by such comments. He has calmly rejected the pig comparison, while at the same time admitting that even if it is true that the Neanderthals possessed the modern apparatus for speech, that does not mean they spoke as we do. That we will never know.

In Chapter Eight we saw that the century-old argument over where the Proto-Indo-Europeans had lived had now come down to a fight over fractures on the surface of some dead horse's teeth. Now we have the century-old battle to determine why the Neanderthals died out focused on a little bone that sat at the back of some caveman's tongue. Seen in this light, the image of medieval theorists debating the number of angels that could be squeezed onto the head of a pin doesn't seem quite so ridiculous.

14

<<<   The Rules of Talk

"Hangubers," "durts," "dits," "baksetball," "mugees," "mulick" and "breafuxt." This is the English that was heard in our house as my two daughters were growing up. "Hangubers" (emphasis on the first syllable) are hamburgers, "durts" is dessert, a "dit" is a drink, "mugees" and "mulick" are both words for music (one for each girl), and "breafuxt" is what both of them eventually decided was a reasonable facsimile of breakfast. And dinner, the meal at the end of the day, was to be eaten when it was "gark" outside.

The amazing thing is that children learn to speak at all. On the one hand, there's the thing you have to learn: language. It's complex in design—very subtly so—and managed by innumerable rules that determine what makes a sentence right. On the other hand, you have the kids down the block, the big sister and the babysitter setting the example of how to use this language! Not to mention the parents: some parents coach, some don't; some use baby-talk, some refuse; there are even some cultures in which it's not thought proper to speak directly to two- or three-year-olds at all. But most kids come through speaking English (or whatever) more or less the way it's supposed to be spoken. Remember, they *never* hear the rules of how they're supposed to speak—they only hear a stream of sounds, and somehow from that they figure out what the rules must be. It's that ease with which something that looks to be so difficult is picked up without any special training that fascinates and frustrates psychologists, linguists, and these days psycholinguists—how do children learn to speak?

Noam Chomsky came up with his idea of a special language organ in the brain partly to explain the ease with which children learn to talk. He argues that this language organ (the existence of which, as we've seen in Chapter Eleven, is by no means unanimously agreed upon) is built in to the brain, like getting a good deal on a computer because it comes with some software packages already included, and that is the reason that children can learn language so easily. Children, according to Chomsky, seem to acquire language out of all proportion to the training they get, and the only reasonable conclusion is that long before they speak, they have the mental equipment to do so, and to do so using all of the grammar, syntax and rules that govern English, French, Kwakiutl or Swahili. It doesn't matter what language a child is trying to learn—the language organ will make it possible.

Since he first went public with these ideas in the 1950s, Chomsky has tinkered with and refined them, and he has now added the idea that as a child learns a specific language, there are the equivalent of on-off switches in the language organ that will be set to adapt the general rules of all human language to the specific rules of that language, and no other. So children in Seoul and Paris are born with the same language organ, but early on the switches are thrown so that one learns Korean, the other French. It's important to remember that being born with a language organ in your brain only gives you the capacity for language (a capacity Chomsky thinks is not present in the great apes); it doesn't ensure that you will learn how to talk. The organ sets down the rules, but you then have to supply the words and ideas.*

---

* Many linguists refer to these rules as *grammar* or *the grammar*, but they're not talking about the seemingly endless rules we learned in school that govern where participles are supposed to go, or how you're not supposed to split an infinitive. Grammar in this general sense is the system for putting words together so that whatever you're saying makes sense to whomever is listening, and that it says exactly what you mean. Some of the words we speak, like "of," "as" and "don't," make the grammar work; others, like "mink," "artillery" and "eyebrow," are the raw materials. And, of course, to do something as simple as chang-

It's one thing to assert that capacity for language resides, as Noam Chomsky insists, in a separate organ or system in the brain (and that children have it from the beginning), but another to find some unambiguous evidence that this is so. However, in the last few years there has been the occasional individual described who, although much below average in mental ability, has developed normal or even sophisticated language skills.[44] One is a girl named Marta who has an IQ in the forties (where normal is about a hundred), but is capable of long, complex and grammatically correct sentences. However, the sentences have unclear meanings, and contain wrong words:

"I haven't shown you my garage yet, but my dad would be really hard."

"I was like fifteen or nineteen when I started moving out o' home, so now I'm like fifteen now, and I can go."

If you ignore the word "hard" in the first sentence, and the confusion of ages in the second, those sentences are perfectly fine—they're put together according to the rules of English. But they don't make much sense. They sound a little like the utterances of people who suffer from Wernicke's aphasia as the result of a stroke, but those people are not retarded in any way. Their problems are

---

ing the order of words in a sentence, you have to follow the strict grammatical rules—if you want it to make sense.

strictly linguistic. Marta is an example of a person who, despite having subnormal mental abilities, still retains perfectly good language.

A more startling example was reported in 1991 in England.[45] A man named Christopher, now in his thirties, scores very badly on some parts of the IQ test, and reportedly has trouble cutting his fingernails or even doing up buttons, yet he has become proficient in sixteen languages! If he's given a passage in any one of them he simply reads it aloud in English at about the speed he'd read English itself. His capacity for learning a new language is frightening: after just two sessions he had learned three hundred words of Hebrew. It's not just that he can learn languages—there has been a handful of people reported over the centuries who were conversant in twenty-five or even more. But most of those were powerful intellects as well; this man, because of apparent brain damage at birth, is not. He performs very badly on tests requiring spatial abilities, like putting together jigsaw puzzle-like shapes. He spent his childhood in schools for the mildly mentally retarded. He is in effect a savant (the term "idiot savant" is now considered inappropriate) for language. Most savants are the reverse—they have very poor language skills, but are phenomenal calculators or musicians.

Christopher and Marta seem to prove that language can be separated out in the brain from other mental abilities, making Noam Chomsky's claim that we all have a separate language organ at least believable. But Chomsky also argues that all children come into the world already possessing this language organ, and so it should be possible to find some evidence of language ability or aptitude (not necessarily the ability to speak) showing up too early in life to have been learned.

Everyone who has spent time with a toddler who is not yet talking has been amazed at how much that child understands of what everybody around her is saying, even though she can't say any of it herself. Experiments in psychology labs have demonstrated that very young babies, only a few months old, already have the ability to tell the difference between sounds that, although differing only very slightly acoustically, play an important role in speech.

A study at the University of Washington tested the ability of six-month-olds to detect the differences among speech sounds.[46] A child would sit in her mother's lap while one of the experimenters sat just off to her right jiggling a little toy up and down to attract the baby's attention. On the left, there was a loudspeaker and a darkened box containing a teddy bear with a drum. The sound of a voice pronouncing a vowel like **ah** came out of the box, but every once in a while it would change to an **ee**. As soon as that happened, the box lit up and the teddy bear banged the drum, and the child would jerk her head around to see what was happening. These babies quickly learned to turn their heads whenever they heard a change in the sounds, knowing that they would soon see the teddy bear and his drum. Then the experiment was made more difficult: the speech sounds were produced by many different voices, with different pitches and sound qualities. The children still had no trouble at all hearing the difference between the two vowels. That experimental set-up has more recently been used to show that by the age of six months, infants are already more familiar with the vowel sounds of their own language than with others, even though they haven't yet learned the meaning of a single word. They're specializing before they talk!

In a second experiment children six months old faced two television monitors, each one with a face on it pronouncing a sound, like **ee** or **ah**. At the same time, they heard one of those sounds coming over the loudspeaker, and more often than not they would look at the correct face, the one making the sound they were hearing. This suggests they already know (unconsciously) the movements necessary to make certain speech sounds, long before they actually start speaking themselves. (Eventually we come to rely heavily on the face to decide what we've actually heard. Adults given a similar test—except that the face and the sound are mismatched—will report hearing the sound the face appears to be making, not the sound that was actually played.)

These early abilities are, however, easily lost. Janet Werker at Dalhousie University and Richard Tees at the University of British Columbia revealed that when six- to eight-month-old children of

English-speaking backgrounds were exposed to sounds in Hindi and Salish (a North American native language), they could tell the difference between the two. But six months later, they had lost that ability. Naturally children speaking Hindi or Salish were still sensitive to the sounds of their respective languages.

An even more dramatic experiment in the 1970s showed that children only *one month old* apparently can hear the difference between **ba** and **pa**— a difference that amounts to a delay of thirty-thousandths of a second in the vibration of the vocal cords. (When you say **ba**, you purse your lips and emit a puff of air at the same time as your vocal cords start to buzz. With **pa**, that buzz is delayed.) One-month-old babies will suck on a nipple (scientists call this the "high-amplitude sucking procedure") as long as they're interested in what's going on around them, and in this experiment, they were played a series of sounds starting with **ba** and then gradually changing to **pa** by delaying the vocal-cord buzz little by little. As the experiment wore on, the babies sucked less and less on the nipple, as they became less and less interested in what seemed to them to be an endless series of the same sound. But suddenly, as the vocal-cord delay reached the thirty-thousandth of a second mark, where we all hear **pa**, not **ba**, the babies suddenly started sucking furiously again.

Do these experiments suggest that babies have the inborn ability to hear speech sounds? Not conclusively—their ability to tell the difference between these speech sounds could have been tuned by listening to their mother's speech inside the womb. But African children have the same reaction, even though they are surrounded in the womb by languages in which these consonants never appear! It looks as if human babies are born with some acute abilities to discriminate between different speech sounds.

A much more important issue than the sound of words is the way they are put together. When children begin to talk, are they using some sort of inborn language organ that governs things like the order and proper usage of words in a sentence?

It's hard to tell at the beginning, mostly because children start with single words at a time, but also because it's often not even clear what is meant by any one word, or even if that sound that seems to be a word really is one. If a father is showing his son a picture of a cat in a book, and his son says, "Ga," does he mean "cat," or is "ga" just something he says when he gets to that page in the book, or is "ga" what seems to be the right response to his father's pointing to that picture and asking, "What's that?"

A twelve-month-old boy named Adam yelled "Dut!" every time he knocked a yellow duck into the bathtub.[47] Most parents would be too busy boring their friends with reports of their son's precocity with language to notice, as the scientists did, that Adam never said "dut" when he just saw the duck sitting on the water, nor did he even say "dut" when someone *else* knocked it into the tub.

The researchers concluded that "dut" was probably Adam's version of "Look out!" or something like that, and couldn't be cited as evidence that he knew that the word "duck" meant that yellow object, no matter where it was, let alone any other duck.

Adam finally learned to say "dut" for all toy ducks, whether he was knocking them into the bath or not, and then he realized the word applied to real ducks. It's not just the problem that the sounds may not mean what you think they mean; there's also the well-established fact that children use a single word to mean many different things, and that doesn't necessarily imply that they don't know what they're doing, or that there is no logical connection among those meanings. "Rain" could indicate that it's raining outside, or that the cat should come in, or that no one will be going out to play. There is a record of a little girl named Eva who used the word "moon" to describe the crescent moon, a piece of crescent-shaped paper, a slice of lemon, a shiny green leaf and cow's horns.[48] All have roughly the same shape, but there was more to Eva's reasoning than that. The lemon slice was about the same colour as the moon, the leaf was shiny, and the cow's horns, at least as seen from below (Eva's perspective), would be superimposed on the sky.

There is also an anecdote of a child who used the word "qua" for a duck swimming on a pond, a cup of milk, a coin with an eagle on it and a teddy bear's eye.[49] At first glance this looks to be a completely indiscriminate use of a word, but the researcher who reported it, the late L.S. Vygotsky, claimed instead that it revealed a fair degree of analysis on the child's part. "Qua" was the duck's quack; then the surrounding pond was linked to the milk in the cup; the duck itself was recognized to be similar to the eagle, then the roundness of the coin on which that eagle was depicted described the roundness of the teddy bear's eye. I don't know how often this kind of definition merry-go-round occurs, but it illustrates just how difficult it can be to be confident about the meaning a child is assigning to the words he or she speaks.

Some linguists have gone as far as to suggest that for children at this early age, single words stand for entire sentences. It's very difficult to know, when a single syllable like **ba** could mean the bath, or "I am in the bath," or "Look! The soap has fallen into the bath." Linguist Ronald Scollon once taped a conversation he'd had with a little girl who could only speak one word at a time, and realized later when he analyzed the tape that she was expressing, in single words like "car," "go" and "bus," that she had heard a car and was reminded that the day before she had had a ride on a bus. In effect she made a multi-word sentence by linking together several one-word utterances.

But as broad as the meanings of single words can be, and as many of them as children know, single words don't make language. Even though some linguists would argue that children speaking a word at a time are already engaged in the practice of assembling language in an order, and are able to understand the detailed architecture of sentences spoken to them (children only seventeen months old can tell the difference between "Big Bird is tickling Cookie Monster," and "Cookie Monster is tickling Big Bird"), most would agree that they are not yet using *language* in the fullest sense of the word. Individual bricks don't mean much to an architect, and while words are much more varied than bricks, it's still more important to see how they're assembled than just to make collections of them. It's when children start using two words at a time that the picture changes completely, because for the first time there's the question of which comes first.

Speaking two words at a time reveals much more about what a child is thinking, and at the same time forces him to be more creative—most two-word utterances are not simple imitations of what he has heard someone else say.

But what then are they? If a child says "Bird fence," is that the shorthand for "There is a bird on the fence" (which is what most of us would assume), or does it simply mean, "There is a bird *and* a fence," a much less interesting statement. One clue to the meaning is to study the order of the words: if they are there just to list what the child sees, they should appear in random order, but if the intention is to locate one on the other, then the order should be more consistent. If a whole series of two-word sentences start with an object (bird, boy, plate, etc.) which is then followed by a location (fence, yard, table), then it's likely that these statements are more than just two words put together. Most studies of these word pairs have confirmed that the children *are* using rules, and that when they appear not to be consistent, it's probably because they are in the midst of refining a rule they've already discovered is inadequate.

But are children at this early age using some sort of formal grammar, or have they just realized that to make other people understand what you're saying, you have to follow some simple rules whenever you put two words together? Are they doing what Noam Chomsky predicted, making guesses (unconsciously) about the rules of English, then gradually refining those guesses as they go along? (All children would have to do this, because even if they were born with a Chomsky language organ, it would be designed to fit all six thousand languages on Earth—the child then has to adjust it to his specific language.) There's certainly no agreement on this, but there is plenty of evidence that children are using rules of some kind—whether they were born with them or just pick them up through learning is another question.

Older children, a little beyond the two-word stage, reveal just how much talk at this still-early stage is guided by rules. When they first start using verbs, they'll often get the irregular ones right: they use "brought," "stood" and "came" where appropriate. But as children's language gets more sophisticated, and they begin to understand the idea of these actions happening in the past, they'll start making mistakes, and say, "bringed," "standed" and "comed." Funnily enough, this is actually progress, because they have invented a new rule for verbs, and they're just being a little overzealous in applying it. At the earlier stage when they were getting these verbs right, they were just learning them on a case-by-case basis—now they have applied a rule. They soon learn that some verbs have to be treated differently, and they start to get it right. Exactly how they learn to correct their mistakes is a mystery: after all, saying "breaked" or "bringed" is actually much more logical and certainly simpler than the adult version, which requires something like 150 exceptions to the rule. And there's no loss of meaning—everyone knows what a child means when she says "bringed." So why do they abandon this system for the more complicated, harder-to-learn adult version? It might be because they are following a predetermined linguistic program. The course of this change has actually been charted with a three-year-old girl named Sally.[50] In December of one year she spoke three verbs that ended in "en": broken, fallen and taken. Then in January "putten" appeared, followed by a flood of "en" words in March and April (most of them invented), including "boughten, builden, riden, getten, wanten, touchen, haden, hurten, leaven, bringen, helpen, spoilen and wasen"—it must have sounded like an SCTV takeoff of an Ingmar Bergman film. These were Sally's version of the past tense. She paused in April, then added nine new ones in May, then only added another four over the rest of the year. At the same time, she was beginning to use the correct past tenses, like "called" instead of "callen," "dripped" instead of "drippen."

It's not clear exactly how Sally (or any other child for that matter) learns that she is overusing the "en" (or the "ed") ending, but the fact that it happens is usually interpreted as a classic example of testing out a rule, then gradually refining it. But what these rules are and where they come from is still a mystery. It's a reflection of the problem of trying to understand something that seems so transparently easy for the children doing it, but so incredibly difficult to the people studying it. In the next chapter, we'll see some of the evidence as to how children go about performing this miracle.

15

How Kids Learn To Talk

The biggest mystery about how children learn to talk is the casualness with which it all proceeds. Parents spend hours talking to their children, but very little of that seems designed to "teach" them how to talk—most of it appears to be unplanned chit-chat that the child somehow picks up, analyzes, then spits back at the surprised parents weeks or even months later. It's exactly because the situation is so unstructured that psychologists and linguists have had so much difficulty pinpointing just how it happens. If it were figure-skating, you could decide that certain moves or exercises make a triple lutz possible, but with talking, it's impossible to do that. The vagueness of it all was one of the factors that prompted Noam Chomsky to argue that so much more language sophistication comes out of a child than goes in, that you have to conclude that they are born with blueprints, plans, software—whatever you want to call it—that enables them to learn as fast as they do.

For instance, as they're learning a language, most children go through exactly the same stages, the only difference being that they reach them at different ages. And these are very well-defined stages, like the ability to use **wh** words, like what, when and where. In this case children, almost all of them, learn first to put these words at the beginning of the sentence: "Where mommy going?" Then they learn to add auxiliary words like "will": "Where you will go? Why kitty can't go?" And finally they understand that some words in the sentence have to change places: "Where will you go? Why can't kitty go?"

Children everywhere seem to learn in this order, and while that doesn't prove Noam Chomsky right, it does give you the feeling of a program unrolling in a predetermined way. Even so, the program, whatever it is, has to be triggered by conversation with others—children don't learn to speak on their own. Yet it is very difficult to gather unambiguous evidence as to what those conversational or social triggers might be.

For instance, there is an assertion that children push themselves to perfect their language because they realize that's the way to get what they want. They begin by using one-word requests ("Cookie"), but after a while single words just aren't enough to convey their ever-growing and increasingly complex set of needs, so they are forced to become more skilful with words. This idea is pretty well summed up in what is an oft-retold story about a couple and their young boy.

These parents were becoming more and more uneasy as time passed and their son spoke not one word. There seemed to be no reason why he wasn't talking: he wasn't deaf, and he seemed to be smart enough. But by the time he had reached the age of four and still hadn't spoken, they began to get desperate. One morning when the whole family was seated at breakfast, he shocked them by saying loudly and clearly, "I didn't get strawberries on my cereal." Even in the midst of her delight and relief, his mother had the presence of mind to ask, "Why have you never spoken before?" to which her son replied, clearly annoyed, "Up till now everything has been all right."

It may never be quite *that* clear-cut, but it makes some sense that children would continue to elaborate on their speech in order to convey their desires more fully and precisely: "Cookie" becomes "I want one of those chocolate cookies in the pantry," and finally "If we're going past the bakery today on the way to swimming could we get a gingerbread man ... please?" All of the complexity of adult English can be recruited to this particular task.

But if a very young child is accomplishing his immediate goals by saying something as simple as "Cookie," why would he keep changing and elaborating that language, going to two words, then strings of words, then short sentences, adding all the structure of correct English, so that he's finally able to come out with "Mommy, can I have a cookie please?" It's hard to prove that the constant pressure to learn how to talk is coming from a desire to articulate better what you want.

And indeed there is evidence that contradicts this idea.[51] A scientific paper published in the late 1970s with the eerie title *Language Without Communication* brought to light the case of a young boy (three years and three months old) named John, whose spoken language seemed at first glance to be more or less normal:

"Nancy is watching the tv."

"What's that bunny rabbit doing?"

"Let's all go inside."

But talk doesn't exist in a vacuum—it's used to communicate. If you take the phrases and short sentences that John spoke, like those above, and see them fitted into their place in the conversation, it becomes clear that he might have been talking, but he wasn't talking *to* anyone. He never spoke at all to anybody other than his parents, and about a third of the time when he was speaking to them he simply ignored what they said. In effect, he was talking to himself:

Father: (referring to a stroller in a book) "Who's in there?"

John: "Read it again."

Father: "Okay. What do you want to read?"

John: "What's that?" (pointing to the book)

This example might not leap out at you as totally aberrant or unusual, but a three-year-old having a normal conversation with a parent would respond to what the father said. Here's another example, recorded when John and his mother were playing a pretend game about driving the car:

Mother: "Are you going to go in and say 'Hi' to Daddy?"

John: "Okay. Here we are in the garage."

John also went to incredible lengths *not* to imitate. If he wanted a green candy and was asked to say, "I want the green one," he would say, "I want the yellow one," or "I want the (pause) green one," or even "I *don't* want the green one." The researchers described as "astonishing" the care with which he avoided repeating exactly what he had heard. Indeed his skill in avoiding imitation underlined the fact that he was very good at perceiving and manipulating words, even though his social use of language was so abnormal. Poor John seemed to have been unaware either of what he was saying, or of what those statements were supposed to do— he didn't seem to have any idea of talk as being part of an exchange of ideas back and forth. He also seemed unable to interpret the gestures that accompany speech (even those as simple as pointing to what's being discussed) or to understand the intent of others around him.

It's not clear why John became this way: his parents were very caring and supportive, and the only hints that something might have been wrong physically were that for some unrecorded reason he was put in an incubator in the hospital when he was two days old, and that he had some problems with his vision. Obviously, even though this is only a single case, it's one that casts doubt on the idea that language progresses only because children are making their needs felt. John's language was advancing, even though it was far from perfect, but he wasn't using it to communicate *any* needs. It's hard to imagine what John's little world must have been like—he was an observer, on the outside looking in, using the appropriate words for the circumstances, yet apparently never realizing that he was part of the scene and others were paying attention to what he was saying and hoping he was paying attention to them.

The story of John suggests that children may not be simply learning to talk to be better at getting what they want, but there is still something crucially important about the interaction between parents and their children. Even John was probably learning *how* to talk from the bizarre "conversations" he was having with his mother and father. And it has to be two-way: simply hearing adult conversation isn't enough. There are several examples of children who have failed to learn to talk even though they have heard a language being spoken for hours at a time on television.

One such little boy, the child of deaf parents, was confined to the house because he was asthmatic, and so didn't hear any appreciable amount of live adult speech until he was three. At that point he was fluent in American Sign Language, but unable to speak, and even when he did learn to speak English, he was unable to put sentences together properly: "I my have home flip-a-coin" meaning "I have a coin at home." Or "Yeah, all finish gimme balloon, you, over there," meaning "Yeah, in the past you gave me a balloon."

Even when children *do* converse with their parents all the time, it's not clear exactly how those conversations help them perfect their language. Some of the clearest evidence downplays the importance of the parent's role: for instance, children tend to ignore parental efforts to correct the mistakes they make, possibly because the rules that they are working with are not yet adult rules, and so don't call for adult sentences:[52]

Child: "Want other one spoon Daddy."

Father (who happened to be a psychologist): "You mean, you want the other spoon."

Child: "Yes I want the other one spoon, please Daddy."

Father: "Can you say, 'The other spoon'?"

Child: "Other ... one ... spoon."

Father: "Say other."

Child: "Other."

Father: "Spoon."

Child: "Spoon."

Father: "Other spoon."

Child: "Other ... spoon. Now give me other one spoon?"

Moreover, even if parents could correct their children successfully, the corrections they tend to make are more often corrections of fact, not grammar. The parental attitude seems to be that if the kid gets the point across, it usually doesn't matter if he's made the verb agree with the subject. But making sure a child knows the difference between a pencil and a pen doesn't help that child on his way to better grammar or more sophisticated sentence structures.

Parents also spend a great deal of time—nearly a third of the time they spend talking to their young children—doing something that some researchers think retards rather than advances their language. It's called "expansion," and it describes the habit of adding onto what a child has just said:

Child: "Dog bark."

Parent: "Yes, the dog is barking, isn't it?"

Apparently parents assume that by adding the little articles and modifiers to a child's two-word effort, the child will soon learn how to speak full-fledged English. In an experiment in which some three-and-a-half-year-olds heard expanded sentences, while others heard sentences that took off from what they'd said and covered new ground, (like "Yes, he's trying to frighten the cat"), those children who heard sentences that covered new ground were, after three months, more advanced: they produced longer, more grammatically complex strings of words.

This experiment may be proving the point that the back-and-forth of conversation is the thing. Children who hear slightly expanded versions of what they have just said themselves aren't getting the benefits of a conversation that moves along. Some linguists have suggested this is the reason behind children asking, "Why?" It's not that they really want to know—they just want to keep the conversation going. When my daughter Amelia was two and a half, she suddenly starting asking "Where?" and the answers were either insufficient, or, as I suspect now, totally irrelevant. When we were in the car she'd ask me where we were going, (home) where? (home) where? (straight ahead) where? (just past that building) where? You could even hear in her tone of voice that she was just waiting until I finished talking before repeating the "where?" I could have said anything and it wouldn't have mattered—she just wanted to talk.

The dispute over exactly what contribution parents make towards teaching their children to talk is best illustrated by the disagreement over the importance of what linguists used to call "motherese," and now, in tune with the times, refer to as "care-giver" language. This is the unique language that most adults use when they speak to young children: it takes the form of baby-talk when the children are very young, but long after the most obvious elements of baby-talk (goo-goo, da-da) have been discarded, adults still speak differently to their children. The debate is over how much influence that special talk has, and how much of a child's language learning is in-built from the beginning.

There's no argument about what care-giver language *is*. When an adult talks to a young child, she slows down, changes her tone of voice, exaggerates her intonation, strips the vocabulary down to a small set of simple words, and (in the case of mothers more than fathers) asks a lot of questions. In baby-talk, the earliest version of care-giver language, it's not just the choice of words that is different—even the sounds are changed and repeated, so that "water" becomes "wa wa," and "train" becomes "choo-choo." Words with lots of consonants in them are even edited ("scambled eggs").

One expert has estimated that as soon as children switch from babbling to talking, adults reduce the complexity of their own grammar to a level only about six months more advanced than the children themselves. This answers one of the apparent puzzles about children learning to talk: how could they learn the simple stuff, when all they were hearing were the long, complex and often ungrammatical ramblings of adults? Simple: that isn't what they hear. Even the subject matter of care-giver language is special: it deals strictly with the here-and-now, not future or past events, and objects, not feelings.

This special language has all the earmarks of something that has evolved over millennia of childcare to be the most effective way to teach children how to talk. But *is* it effective? That's where the controversy is today, and like so many other linguistic debates, this one revolves around the ideas of Noam Chomsky. Chomskyites believe that children learn language at pretty much their own self-determined pace, regardless of how many times they hear "tum-tum" and "boo-boo," because the important determinants of language learning are built in. Their opponents argue that, to the contrary, the care-giver's role is so important that it makes a mockery of the idea that progress depends on some sort of child's language learning organ; instead, we should think of a mother's (or father's) innate language *teaching* ability.

Researchers such as the Oxford psychologist Jerome Bruner have claimed that it's the interaction between adult and child that is the important thing, and that by the time a child is just beginning to speak, that give-and-take relationship has already been worked out.[53] The adult uses baby talk primarily to keep the two of them focused on the same topic, but while the content may be infantile, the exchange is adult, and it's the details of that exchange that fuel the learning. Mothers who have been watched as they talk to their children always use a fixed order in what they say. "Look, what's that?" then, "That's a duck," then (in response to the child repeating the word "duck"), "That's right." Once they have that routine down, the mother ups the ante: if the child just smiles when he looks at what she's pointing at, she gives it a name. But if it appears he might name it himself, she waits. She uses different voices for things he already knows and things she suspects he doesn't yet know—she always seems to be prodding and pushing the child to develop his or her language skills.

Jerome Bruner argues that much of what's going on is establishing, then developing the roles the child and his mother play, and that these in turn help teach some of the subtleties of language. As the child gets older, there are variations in roles: in some situations, like reading, the child is the

recipient; in some, like peekaboo, there is turn-taking; and sometimes they take equal roles, as when
they are going for a walk together. Understanding
different roles could be a first step towards understanding difficult concepts in language like the fact
that you can be either "you" or "I," depending on
who is speaking.

It makes sense that adults would only go to the
trouble of creating a unique language for their children if it worked—if it really helped children learn
to talk faster and better. But there are studies that
have raised doubts about care-giver language, and
at the very least suggest that the good it's doing is a
lot more subtle than expected.

For instance, Henry and Lila Gleitman and
Elissa Newport in the United States have shown
that the importance of the simplicity of the sentences adults use with children has been over-
played.[54] They argue that much of the reduction of
complexity has nothing to do with teaching the
child how to speak, and everything to do with
making sure that the child and the care-giver are
talking about the same thing, and that the child is
paying attention (and of course that the child will
do what the care-giver wants, and now!). So only a
few topics are ever addressed, and the child's limited attention span is taken into account by speaking slowly, clearly and briefly. These can be (and
are, according to these researchers) mistaken for
attempts to teach the language by beginning with
simple versions of it—in fact, there seems to be no
correlation between these features of an adult's

language and the development of the child's linguistic ability. As well, care-givers use more kinds of sentences, with more inconsistency in their structure, when they're talking to their children than when they're talking to adults! Another peculiarity of care-giver language is that the adult's way of talking stays pretty much the same, even while the child is becoming more and more sophisticated linguistically.

Nevertheless, there are some features of care-giver language that do help children learn English, and these are features that at first glance might have seemed to be no help at all. For instance, adults spend much more of their time giving children orders and asking them questions than they do using the simple sort of sentences they tend to use with adults. A sentence like "Rachel wants an apple" is common in adult-to-adult conversation, but care-giver language contains many more questions and orders ("Do you want an apple?" "Eat that apple, please.") than simple declarations.

Even though these seem much more difficult, if only because the word order is twisted around from the usual, it seems as if children learn to use words that go along with verbs (like "can," "will" and "do") faster if the adult is asking them a lot of questions that demand yes or no answers, or even giving them orders (*don't* sing). The Gleitmans and Elissa Newport suggest this is because children pay better attention to the first word in a sentence, and in yes-no questions, the first word is usually one of those helper words, like can or will.

So at least in this study it appeared that in some ways children can learn words that play an important role in grammar faster if they are constantly hearing certain kinds of sentences. On the other hand, care-giver language seemed to be very little help at all in expanding a child's vocabulary of concrete nouns and verbs. Here is another sign that not all words are equal, at least in our brains. Other research, unrelated to the question of how children learn to talk, has shown that the left front part of the brain reacts to the sight of these grammar words (like "can," "will," and "if") but not to the sight of words like "zebra," "townhouse" or "ankle." People with Broca's aphasia have trouble both producing and comprehending those grammar words. Here there's evidence that care-giver language influences how fast children learn the grammar words, but not the concrete words.

The bottom line is, as in just about every other area of linguistic research, that nobody really knows just how important care-giver language is, or exactly how much it does, or even when. One recent suggestion is that it may be most important at a much earlier age than most experiments have surveyed. The extraordinary ability of six-month-old children to distinguish among the vowel sounds of their own language—even before they learn what the words mean—might be made possible by care-giver language. The slow, clear pronunciation could help infants identify ideal examples of vowel sounds.

To recap: it's not safe to assume that the efforts

to which adults go to ensure that children learn to talk are always effective. Children ignore corrections, and in one study seemed not to benefit at all from so-called "expansions," when an adult simply adds to what the child has just said. "Caregiver" language too is not all that it might seem. Its simplicity can be seen as an attempt to get the point across, rather than ensuring future fluency, and it may be that only very specific abilities, like being able to use words such as "can," "will" and "do" with verbs, are fostered by care-giver language. It doesn't seem to have much influence on how quickly a child learns concrete nouns and verbs.

The best way to make sense of all this is to assume that some of language learning, or at least a capacity for learning, is innate: a child brings her own unconscious and automatic abilities with her. Perhaps the rest is dependent on interactions with the people around her; perhaps even the innate programs themselves remain inert unless they too are stimulated by conversation. It only takes about three or four years from the time a child first tries the odd word until she has learned to apply all the rules and is using language at an adult level. Usually a simple and painless process, yet no computer has been programmed to produce sentences that obey all the grammatical rules learned during this time. What is probably true, though, is that if the rules *aren't* learned during that time, or at least in the next few years, a child may never learn to talk.

16

<<< The Wild Children

In the early morning of January 9, 1800, a strange creature appeared out of the woods near the French village of Saint-Sernin, in the district of Aveyron, one hundred and twenty-five kilometres north of the Spanish border.[55] He appeared to be a small boy, but he acted like a wild animal. He was caught digging up vegetables from a tanner's garden, and was soon turned over to a local official, who made some notes about him.

He was about four feet tall, and although he was wearing a tattered shirt, his behaviour made it apparent that he had been roaming the countryside, apart from civilization, for some time. He rejected all food offered him except some potatoes, which he threw into the open fire, later picking them out *with his bare hands* and eating them immediately!* He refused wine, accepted some water, then tried to run away, but showed no resentment at being recaptured.

Perhaps the oddest thing was that he couldn't speak; the only sounds he made were strange cries. Even though he had a deep scar across his throat, he seemed physically capable of speaking—he just didn't. This was the Wild Boy of Aveyron, the "Wild Child" of François Truffaut's 1969 movie.

As the word of his capture spread, there came proof that this boy, who was probably twelve years old, had been running wild for at least three years, and probably more. People in a town more than a hundred kilometres away had seen him two or three years earlier in and out of the woods, eating acorns and roots. He had been captured once or twice, had learned to cook potatoes in a fire, and had been clothed on one occasion, accounting for the tattered shirt he was wearing when he turned up in Aveyron. The striking thing was that he had developed an easy-going relationship with the people in the area. They let him come into their

---

* This was only one example of his insensitivity to extreme temperatures—he could just as easily roll around in the snow unclothed, apparently in perfect comfort. Oddly enough, a modern "wild child," the girl Genie in California, had the same sort of tolerance to heat and cold when she was first discovered.

homes and eat, then return unhindered to the woods. But this live-and-let-live situation ended abruptly when the boy was captured in 1800—he never ran free again.

When the news reached Paris, the social scientists and philosophers became very interested in the wild boy, because he could be used to test some of the popular theories of the day about human nature: would he reveal an innate human consciousness like that of our ancient ancestors, before there was language and education? Or would he be a blank slate, exhibiting nothing of human intelligence and culture because of having lived outside society? The wild child was, at least in the eyes of the Parisian intellectuals, an inadvertent experiment that might address some of the central philosophical issues of the day, and they wanted to get a look at him firsthand.

He was taken by stagecoach to Paris, but his rehabilitation got off to a very rough start. In his first few weeks, probably disoriented, he became more and more anti-social, and a committee of experts dismissed him as an idiot, and therefore uninteresting as an experiment. If he hadn't sparked the interest of Dr Jean-Marc Itard, the wild boy may well have been left to live out his days in the Institute for Deaf-Mutes, unwatched and unattended.

Itard was a doctor at the Institute, and just when everyone else had abandoned interest in the wild child, Itard took him over. It's not clear why he thought the boy was worth working with, especially since the much more experienced and illustrious experts at the Institute had written him off. But Itard decided he would try to train the child's senses, to teach him to think clearly, and to speak.

The story of Itard and the boy, whom he named Victor, is an emotional one of a clinician who devoted six of his most productive years to the single task of bringing out the humanness in Victor. He had mixed success: the boy eventually learned how to read and write simple sentences, and that, together with other evidence of his intelligence, made it clear that whatever Victor was, he wasn't an idiot.

On the other hand, Itard not only was never able to teach Victor to speak, he never even came close. Early on in their relationship Itard was delighted when Victor said the word "*lait*" when presented with a glass of milk. But, as Itard later realized, it's not enough to have the word and the glass at the same time. Victor could have been using the word "*lait*" (which Itard had been trying to teach him) simply as an expression of delight. He almost never said the word *before* getting the glass, as he would have had to if he were asking for the milk. He never used the word when the milk wasn't right in front of him, nor did he ever make it clear that he understood what "*lait*" meant. These crucial flaws in what had seemed to be an early triumph made Itard realize that speech was going to be very difficult to achieve. Eventually Victor learned to say the expression "*Oh Dieu*," and a few isolated vowels and consonants. But that was all he ever said.

But that didn't mean that Victor couldn't acquire some kind of language. Itard persisted and finally, after months and months of intensive one-on-one training, Victor was able to associate some printed words with the objects they represented. Dr Itard would place a few common objects like a book, a key and a knife in his study, then move to another room with Victor. Itard would point to the names of these objects and ask Victor to go to the study and get them. Victor had no problems with this test, until one day when Itard locked the study door. Victor returned empty-handed, and Itard then pretended he couldn't find the key, and asked Victor to find the same objects around him. The particular objects Victor was to retrieve that day were a stick, bellows, brush, glass and knife, examples of all of which were in plain view in the room. If Victor recognized that these were the same kinds of things as the objects behind the locked study door, it would demonstrate that he understood that the word "stick" meant *all* sticks, not just the one he had been trained with. But he couldn't do it, even when Itard suggested—by gestures—that he look around and see if there weren't objects around him just like the ones he was supposed to be retrieving. The wild child was seeing differences instead of similarities—apparently every knife looked slightly different to him, so it didn't make sense to choose one when he knew the other wasn't the same.

It's important to remember that even though Victor was now a teenager, he was making the same kinds of linguistic mistakes as normal children two or three years old, a measure of just how far he'd been set back by his years in the wild.

But even he began to realize that a word could stand as a symbol for a set of objects, and from there he went on to grasp the idea of words that weren't the names for objects, words like "big," "little," "hot," "cold" and "heavy." Itard wrote that Victor was able to "use his writing, crude as it is, to express his needs, to ask for what he wants."

That was in 1803, and still Victor couldn't speak. Itard, who had worked on developing Victor's reading and writing after his initial disappointments in teaching him to talk, returned to his goal of making Victor capable of conversation, and in a display of incredible tenacity and faith, spent more than a year trying to teach Victor to imitate the movements of face, lips and tongue that Itard made when he articulated speech sounds. But still all Victor could manage was a few indistinguishable monosyllables, and finally Itard became convinced that Victor would never be able either to perceive or produce speech sounds.

This was a defeat from which the doctor never recovered—although speech was only one of many human attributes that Itard was trying to reawaken (or create) in Victor—and shortly after he abandoned his efforts to get Victor to speak, Itard stopped working with Victor, and went on to other research. Victor continued to live in Paris, although in near obscurity and with no further training. The legendary wild child died in 1828, no longer a child, but not really an adult; no longer wild, but not completely civilized either.

Victor's story is one that linguists today still find fascinating, because a child in his circumstances might provide confirmation for the theory that there is a critical period during which a child must learn language—it won't happen before or after. If, for whatever reason, a child misses that critical period, at the very least he will never be able to use language as well as he should, or at worst, will never learn proper language at all.

The critical period may be fairly long—one suggestion is from the age of two to puberty—but both before and after that period, the assumption is that the brain either isn't yet fully developed enough to be able to learn language, or has passed its peak for language and can only acquire it half-heartedly. There's plenty of evidence from experiments with other animals and birds that there are such sensitive periods, especially early in life. The nervous system and the brain are continuously developing, and windows for certain abilities open, then close, and unless the animal has the appropriate experience during that time, it may never acquire that ability. If kittens are only able to use one eye between the ages of four and twelve weeks, they will never develop the nerve connections in the brain that make binocular (stereoscopic) vision possible. A kitten which is restricted to seeing only vertical stripes during this period, even if only for a few days, will never be able to jump onto the seat of a chair, because it will not be able to perceive horizontal surfaces—it literally can't see the chair seat. Birds raised in isolation never learn the song that is characteristic of their species.

There is some evidence in humans as well: studies of deaf children born to hearing parents and exposed to American Sign Language at different ages have revealed that the ability to use sign language is dependent on when it was first learned. (The assumption here, which most linguists would accept, is that the same sort of language learning goes on whether you're learning to speak or sign.) It's also true that learning a second language is much easier, and much more accurate, the earlier it's done, although it should be noted that some have argued that these data don't show anything more than the ability of a young and flexible brain to learn new things.

It's not possible to confirm or deny the idea of a critical period from Victor's story, as detailed as Dr Itard's reports were, because no one knows how he became wild in the first place. If he had lived with adults for two or three years before he ran free, he could have begun to learn to speak then, and that initial period would have influenced what Victor was able to learn under Dr Itard's direction. Itard has also been criticized for not capitalizing on Victor's accomplishments with reading and writing to push his linguistic accomplishments further. For some reason, Itard had fixed on spoken language as the only legitimate goal. The irony was that, though Victor was being trained in the Institute for Deaf-Mutes, Itard never tried to teach him sign language. Victor remains today one of the most tantalizing of all stories of people deprived of language, but there just isn't quite enough information about him to draw many conclusions.*

There has been nothing exactly like the "wild child" in recent times, but a rough parallel, a story of almost unimaginable cruelty, surfaced in Cali-

---

* The strangest story of language disability caused by lack of contact with other people is that of Alexander Selkirk, a Scottish sailor who was marooned on an island off the coast of Chile in 1704. He spent four years and four months alone on this island before being discovered by an English pirate ship. Selkirk's experience was probably the inspiration for Daniel Defoe's Robinson Crusoe, although Defoe added twenty-four years and one Friday. The captain of the British ship who found Selkirk, Woodes Rogers, wrote in his diary that Selkirk had "almost entirely forgotten the secret of articulating intelligible sounds" even though he had had some books on the island with him. Apparently what speech he'd retained could scarcely be understood. This of course is not a parallel to the wild child, in that Selkirk was already able to speak English perfectly well when he was marooned, and whatever language ability he had was lost over the four years. It seems unbelievable, given that hostages were held in Beirut in the 1980s for at least that length of time, some of them with apparently no verbal contact with anyone, yet were extremely articulate, almost verbose, when they were released. As intriguing as the Selkirk story is, it can't tell us very much about language.

fornia in 1970.[56] The victim, a girl named Genie, has shown not only how the human spirit can survive in the face of the most horrible circumstances, but also what happens to a child's language if she is never given a chance to learn it.

Genie's father was psychotic, and intensely jealous of the attention Genie's mother was paying to the little girl, so he confined Genie to an empty room at the back of their house. (He also apparently feared the exploitation that Genie, whom he thought to be retarded, might face.) She was kept strapped to a potty chair during the day, able to move only her feet and hands, and at night she slept in a sleeping bag to which he had attached a harness, making it into a kind of strait-jacket, which was then lowered into a crib with wire-mesh sides and a wire-mesh cover.

The father kept a wooden board in the room to beat Genie whenever she made any noise, so she learned never to talk or cry out. Even if she made some noise with her body, he would beat her. He gave up speaking to her—instead he barked and snarled like a dog. He would often stand outside her door and growl threateningly. That was the sound that Genie probably heard most as she grew up. Her father trained her elder brother to growl too, and he took over much of the girl's care because her mother was going blind. Genie was only allowed to eat baby foods, cereal and the occasional soft-boiled egg, with the result that even years after she was freed from her parents and was living in a foster home, she wouldn't chew her food, but would simply allow it to sit in her mouth until it became soft enough to swallow.

Genie was discovered only when her mother, who was also beaten repeatedly by the father and lived in constant fear of him, finally left him after an especially violent argument. A few weeks after that, when the mother took Genie with her to apply for aid for the blind, they inadvertently ended up in a family aid building. Staff there immediately realized there was something seriously wrong: they saw a thirteen-and-a-half-year-old girl who weighed fifty-nine pounds, couldn't walk properly, couldn't stand erect, and could only whimper. It was a miracle that she was alive, and as it turned out, sane. (Her father committed suicide the day he was to go to trial for his mistreatment of her.) Unlike hostages, she couldn't dream of being released from the horror in which she lived, because she knew no alternative. There was no television or radio in the house, and she saw virtually nobody except her family. And yet, Genie had somehow, unbelievably, kept her spirit.

She spent months in hospital, then was eventually moved to a foster home. Genie gradually changed from a creature who was, in many ways, as inhuman as the wild child, into an adolescent girl. But she never became "normal." As the years passed, and the linguist who was studying her, Dr Susan Curtiss, continued to monitor Genie's abilities, it became clear that Genie's language wasn't retarded across the board, but was mixed: very slow in some ways, close to normal in others.

Sorting out those differences has led to some unexpected conclusions about how we learn to talk.

As parents are acutely aware, children begin asking questions practically as soon as they start talking. They create those questions first by changing their tone of voice, then by using words like "when" and "where," and finally by adding to both of those the really sophisticated tricks of changing the order of words in the sentence. Genie couldn't do any of these. It was in response to concerted efforts to get her to use the **wh** words that she produced some of her most confused sentences: "Where is may I have a penny?" and "I where is graham cracker on top shelf?" She was also unable to master the use of pronouns like "he."

Teacher: "Give me a 'he' sentence. Start it with 'he' and tell me about the boy in the picture."

Genie: "The boy signing is he cookie."

In addition to "he," Genie never was able to use "you" or "me" either. In fact, she never appeared to learn any of the conventional expressions that lubricate normal conversations, like "Hi, how are you," "Please," "Okay," or even the little words and phrases like "Well," or "And then."

But it wasn't always the case that Genie lacked some feature of adult English. She occasionally invented new kinds of English, such as the following sentences where a single noun—like "cat" in the first example—plays a dual role: the object of one verb and the subject of the next: "Ruth Smith have cat swallow needle."

Or sadly, "Father hit Genie cry longtime ago."

Children learning to speak always understand more words than they can produce—how many times have parents suddenly become aware that a young child knows exactly what they're talking about, even though that child can't repeat a word of it? In Genie's case, however, the gap between understanding and speaking was much greater than normal. Most of the architecture of English, especially grammar, posed absolutely no problem for her when it appeared in the speech of others, but she could never produce it herself.

The puzzle of Genie was not so much that at the age of fourteen her language was so limited, or that even after several years of relatively normal life there were still many features of language that apparently she would never be able to learn. With the appalling conditions she had lived with, and the abuse she had suffered, it was a wonder that she could even *approach* being normal. And in some surprising ways, Genie was mentally superior to the rest of us. Even though she always had problems counting, even to five, she had an almost unconscious ability to sense numbers: asked to get five napkins, Genie could reach into a pile and grab exactly five, apparently without thinking, and certainly without counting. This ability to judge numbers was only one of a set of abilities that indicated that Genie had an unusual capacity for dealing with the parts of things compared to the wholes.

In tests where Genie was asked to identify the subject of pictures or silhouettes which had parts missing or hidden, she scored higher than most adults. In one of these tests she scored near the maximum possible on the test. In another, called the Mooney Faces Test, the goal is to identify which out of the total of seventy black-and-white splotches are the fifty that have been derived from line drawings of faces, and which are the twenty that are just randomly arranged patches. Usually only sixty faces are used in the test, because there are ten which are rarely identified correctly. Genie was given all seventy, and she correctly identified fifty out of fifty real faces, and fourteen of the twenty false faces. She scored higher on this test than *anybody ever has.*

Susan Curtiss, who worked so closely with Genie in the years after she escaped her father, recognized that Genie's extraordinary abilities in tests like the identification of the Mooney Faces, coupled with her very poor language ability, said something unexpected about her brain: Genie was a right-brained person. The ability to recognize faces and to imagine the whole picture when presented with only a part are tasks performed best by the right cerebral hemisphere. But that same hemisphere is very unskilled at language—the main language centres are of course on the left side, the left cerebral hemisphere.

Susan Curtiss was able to test the idea that Genie was relying almost entirely on her right hemisphere by presenting a different word to each of Genie's ears (through headphones) at exactly the same time. Genie would hear the instruction "Point to the ___ " through both ears, but each ear would hear a different word. Whichever object Genie pointed to on the page in front of her would be the word she heard best. The ears feed the sounds they collect first and principally to the opposite hemisphere in the brain, so normally a right-handed adult (with language in the left hemisphere) will point more often to the word that was fed into their right ear. The advantage of one ear over the other isn't usually very large, but in Genie's case it was enormous. Her left ear—and so her right hemisphere—was completely dominant. Her scores were as lopsided as those seen with people who only have a right hemisphere (following surgery to remove the left hemisphere, usually because of a malignant tumour). She performed on these tests as if a right hemisphere was all she had! But it wasn't just these listening tests. Most of Genie's language problems—the inability to use **wh** words, much better comprehension than production, retarded development—are typical of adults who have lost their left hemisphere through surgery and have to learn language all over again with their right hemisphere. These inabilities are also typical of children who are just starting to speak. (And a third group—chimpanzees—show some of the same shortcomings in language.)

Could the brain's left hemisphere be the common factor in all of these? What if the so-called "critical period" were a time when the left hemisphere was receptive to language? It could be that very young children with an immature left hemisphere are too early for full-fledged language (even though they might know all kinds of words) and adults (like those who have just had their left hemisphere removed) are too late. And Genie was too late too—the fact that her left hemisphere didn't take over when she began learning language might mean that she had missed the critical period. And if that time is missed, the left hemisphere may be incapable of *ever* learning language.*

Theorists like to read into the case of Genie whatever they want to see. Some linguists don't accept the idea that there is a critical period for

---

* Dr Helen Neville's work (as described in Chapter Five) showing how the left front part of the brain responds electrically to the sight of grammar words like "as," "with" and "or" (but not to nouns or verbs) bears directly on this question. She's found that people deaf from birth show no such response—their brains have literally become organized differently as a result of not acquiring spoken language as most hearing people do. Her findings can be interpreted to mean that the left hemisphere must be exposed to conversation early for normal language development. But more than that, it suggests that without that early exposure, the brain itself won't become organized into the usual left-right split. It's not that the usual language hemisphere, the left, will remain blank—it will actually lose its capacity for language, and possibly other mental abilities, and the brain will become organized in a completely different way than it would have been had that individual been exposed to language at an early age. Our brains have a right-left difference, not *for* language, but *because* of it.

learning a language, and so deny that Genie is good evidence for it—they argue that her complete reliance on her right hemisphere may be an abnormal situation, and that in effect she had suffered some sort of brain damage. And besides, they add, one case does not make a theory. Susan Curtiss points out that one case or not, Genie is the best example we have of someone who might have missed the critical period for learning to talk. This is one situation where no one would regret the small number of people to study.

Genie has attracted the attention of the University of Hawaii linguist Derek Bickerton too. He thinks that there are two kinds of language, the full-fledged adult version, and a primitive so-called "proto-language" that some humans under the age of two and chimpanzees use, and he argues that Genie acquired the latter, but wasn't able (despite intensive training) to progress further than that. In fact, Bickerton thinks there must have been a time in our evolution when all we *had* was the simple, Genie kind of language. Then there was a change, some sort of miraculous gene mutation that affected only the left hemisphere, and conferred on it the ability to perceive and produce language in its fullest form, leaving the right hemisphere stuck back at the earlier linguistic stage. According to this version of the evolution of language, adults who have had their left hemisphere removed, and tragic cases like Genie, are people who have travelled back in time to when the only talk we were capable of was the simple, not-quite language they speak.

Genie lives today in an institution in California, a place that can't provide anything like the stimulation she received when Susan Curtiss was working with her. At last word, her language skills have declined dramatically since the 1970s. Both she and Victor were, for a few years, the subject of intensive study and emotional support. But for both, those times changed, and it's likely Genie will die almost unnoticed, just like Victor, the Wild Boy of Aveyron.*

---

* The case of Genie has many more twists and turns than I have mentioned here. A two-part article in *The New Yorker* in April 1992, by Russ Rymer, called "A Silent Childhood," makes clear just how tragic Genie's story continues to be. Genie's mother, Irene, was angered by the publication of Susan Curtiss's book in 1977, because she felt it contained information about Genie's life at home that could only have been acquired from records of her private sessions with her therapist. She filed suit in 1979 against several of those involved in Genie's rehabilitation, charging, among other things, violation of confidentiality and performing "extreme" and "unreasonable" experiments on Genie. The case dragged on until 1984, and when the court decided in the end that Irene had no right to prevent the scientists from being in contact with her daughter, she sent Genie away to the home where she now lives. Only one of the original team knows where she is. Susan Curtiss hasn't seen Genie for several years.

17

<<<   Talk, Talk (Growl), Talk

A canine movie star was one of the first animals to
be tested for the ability to understand human
speech.[57] During the 1920s Fellow, a German
Shepherd, was very big in movies that called for
the rescue of small children from rushing rivers
and the like. According to his owner, the dog
understood four hundred words of English. This is
the sort of claim that you read these days while
standing in the supermarket checkout line, but the
case of Fellow was different, because two psychologists, C.J. Warden and L.H. Warner, conducted a
series of tests to see just how good Fellow was. In
these tests (which were designed to see if the dog
would do exactly what he was told) both the
owner, Jacob Herbert, and the psychologists were
quite aware of the pitfalls, and they took special
steps to eliminate any subtle cues that Mr Herbert
might be using to signal Fellow, unwittingly or

not.* There was a distinct danger of this happening with Fellow, because his owner was the only person from whom he would take commands.

The first set of experiments was held in a New York hotel suite, with Mr Herbert giving commands from behind the closed bathroom door. The psychologists sat in the room with the dog, but took care not to give Fellow any information that might lead him to respond correctly to a command. Fellow did well enough (especially considering that was probably the first time he'd had to respond to a command when his owner couldn't be seen) that a second set of tests was scheduled, in the psychology lab at Columbia University in

---

* This is a phenomenon that has come to be known as The Clever Hans Effect. Hans was a horse who wowed Berliners at the turn of the century with his ability to do mental arithmetic. He would work his way through complicated addition and subtraction problems, tapping his hoof to indicate the correct answer. It was finally shown that Hans' trainer, Wilhelm von Osten, was unconsciously giving the answers away: he would stand completely still as the horse pawed away at the ground, until Hans reached the right number, at which point he would give a slight shrug of his shoulders, or twitch his eyebrows; Hans would see this and stop counting. The Clever Hans Effect now means something slightly broader: experimenters, anxious for their animals to be successful, becoming too lax in eliminating the possibility that the humans are somehow cueing the answers.

New York.

This time all three people were hidden behind screens. The results were interesting: Fellow had little trouble with commands like "stand still, roll over, turn your head ... (now turn) the other way, take care of him (Fellow assumes a protective attitude), close your mouth, look up high." He responded correctly to fifty-three commands like this, even with his master hidden behind a screen. But these were all commands that could be done on the spot—when Fellow had to move to a different place, or approach an object, as with "Go in the other room and get my gloves," or "Go and look out the window," he had trouble, even though these were commands he normally obeyed with ease and accuracy. Then Warner and Warden allowed Herbert to be present when he gave these commands, but had him looking away, or facing the wrong direction when he did. Fellow was stumped again. It became obvious he could form some associations between words and acts or objects, but as the demands became more complicated, he needed more than just the clues he got from the words.

The experiments with Fellow illustrate something important: when an animal appears to have a good knowledge of a language, it's very important to identify what sorts of extra information he's taking in besides the words.

There are no researchers today who think that dogs can understand English (in the fullest sense of understanding), but several think that apes can.

The question of whether chimpanzees or gorillas can learn a language was hot in the 1960s and 1970s, cooled off dramatically in the 1980s, but has heated up again. It's a subject where vicious putdowns and scorn pass for academic debate, probably because the suggestion that apes might be capable of language strikes at the definition of what it is to be human. Language is one of the few things left that is—or may be—unique to our species.

There were a couple of attempts earlier in this century to teach chimpanzees to talk, but they failed for the simple reason that chimpanzees don't have the vocal anatomy to make the sounds needed for, say, English. They can make a variety of noises, but they can't talk. That doesn't mean they can't understand and use a language, and this research really took off when scientists began teaching chimpanzees to use symbols, rather than words. One project that began in the 1960s involved teaching a chimp named Washoe how to make the signs of American Sign Language, while another chimp, Sarah, was taught to use plastic symbols with magnets on the back that could be stuck to a board.

These experiments were very exciting. These chimpanzees soon made it clear that they understood that a sign made with the hands or a piece of plastic could stand for something else. Washoe, the chimp using American Sign Language, learned more than a hundred signs, words like gimme, hurry, tickle and toothbrush, and was capable of using them in different situations. Once Washoe saw a glass with toothbrushes in it in a bathroom, and made the sign for toothbrush, even though she wasn't asking for them, nor wanted her teeth brushed, a procedure she disliked intensely. She just knew that the sign "meant" toothbrush.

But even more impressive, Washoe seemed to be capable of putting symbols in an order that meant something—creating short, simple sentences in the same way that children do. She invented sequences like "Hurry gimme toothbrush," or "Roger Washoe tickle." The proof that these were a set of signs that she intended to be interpreted together was that she didn't drop her hands from the signing position until she was finished. There were even times when it appeared as if she was inventing labels: in what has become a famous example, Washoe saw a swan on a pond, and put together the two symbols for "water" and "bird." "Water bird." These were dramatic steps forward, and it began to look as if it were only a matter of time and teaching before Washoe would show that the amazing feat of learning to talk is not necessarily limited to our species.

Sarah, the chimp using the plastic symbols, learned language completely differently. Instead of being allowed to move around freely and playing with people, like Washoe, Sarah was kept in a cage and trained to use her symbols to solve problems. She became quite accomplished: if she were shown a set of symbols like "If apple, then chocolate," she would take the apple first in anticipation of getting some of her favourite treat, chocolate. If asked to put "Green on red" she could put a green symbol on top of a red one. She apparently mastered the idea of same or different, by matching the right symbol for one of those with a pair of objects that were indeed the same or different. She could also match half an apple with half a glass of water, implying, at least to her teacher David Premack, that not only could she mentally reconstruct a whole apple or a full glass, but that she understood what half meant, and could apply the concept to different things. On the other hand, Sarah's language was used only in narrowly defined ways: she never had conversations with her trainers as Washoe did.*

---

* There is also Koko, a famous gorilla, that has learned, in American Sign Language, something like six hundred words that she uses in her everyday conversation. Now she even uses an Apple Mac II computer to make the audible spoken version of symbols that she presses on the screen. Koko became famous, not for her language skills, but for her much-publicized anguish when her pet kitten was accidentally killed, and her subsequent joy at getting a new one. It's even been claimed that Koko scores just below the human average on a standard IQ test. She has invented novel sign combinations, like "white tiger" for "zebra," "cookie rock" for "stale bun," and "fruit lollipop" for "frozen banana," and she once had the following conversation with her trainer, Dr Penny Patterson:
"Sorry bit scratch wrong bite."
"Why bite?"

Through the 1970s, the research with ape language went from triumph to triumph. Then, in 1979, it appeared to come crashing down.[58] Dr Herbert Terrace, a researcher at Columbia University who had been working with his own chimpanzee, Neam Chimpsky (cute eh?), published a report in the influential magazine *Science* debunking the entire enterprise. On the basis of his analysis of what his chimpanzee (whose name became abbreviated to Nim) was capable of, Terrace and his colleagues decided that most of the claims made by other researchers were illusion, that the strings of signs or symbols put together by these animals were imitation, repetition or simply individual signs assembled in a random order, none of which said anything about the animals' ability to produce what researchers would accept as true language.

Terrace's approach was to tape everything that Nim produced and then analyze it later, and he collected a huge body of material, something like 20,000 sequences of signs. (Nim too learned the chimp version of American Sign Language.) More than half of those twenty thousand were sequences

---

"Because mad."

"Why mad?"

"Don't know."

(F. Patterson and R. Cohn, "Language Acquisition by a Lowland Gorilla: Koko's First Ten Years of Vocabulary Development," *Word* 41 (1990): 97–143)

of two or more signs, and while many of those were identical ("eat Nim" showed up more than three hundred times; "Nim eat" more than two hundred), there were still well over a thousand sequences that were different from each other. On the plus side, there was evidence that Nim preferred certain orders of words: when he used the sign for "more," eighty percent of the time it preceded the word it modified, as in "more tickle," or "more drink." Herbert Terrace allowed that this provided "superficial evidence" that Nim was following some rules for word order. But he went on to point out that all the other evidence made this unlikely. For one thing the length of Nim's statements averaged between about one sign and one sign and a half for the nineteen months of his training, even though at the same time his vocabulary tripled from 42 to 125 signs. Furthermore, his combinations of three signs showed no sign of any regularity in order, and more important, they added nothing to the information already available from two-sign messages. For instance, "Me Nim food eat" is really nothing more than "food eat": adding "Nim" and "me" is unimportant because Nim never referred to anyone but himself anyway, nor did he talk about anything much other than food. In this Nim seemed to be very different from young children: they understand that food can be for the cat or their sister. Nim also produced more and more imitations (making a certain sign immediately after one of his trainers had made it) as he got older, while children make fewer.

Herbert Terrace felt after all this analysis that the key difference between Nim and a child was that the child would participate in a conversation and contribute to moving the exchange along, but Nim couldn't. (Koko the gorilla sounds as though she's holding up her end of the conversation quoted earlier in this chapter, but Terrace still argues that apes can't master language.) He also claimed that the other apparently more successful experiments with chimps were plagued by unnoticed imitation—that these chimps often were making the same signs that the trainer had just made, sometimes with prompting, sometimes not, meaning that some statements that had been judged to be spontaneous and creative were nothing of the sort. He also argued that in situations where it appeared that a chimpanzee had understood the meaning of questions like "What that?" or "Colour that?" the amount of drilling the animals had had, and the limited number of possible answers, like two, made it impossible to make any claims for linguistic ability. Terrace felt that chimps had to demonstrate an understanding of the symbols they were using far beyond what had been shown.

One of the most widely quoted examples of the chimp Washoe's ability to create new combinations of signs was the previously mentioned "water bird." Terrace, in his devastating critique of chimp language in 1979, questioned just what it meant. He argued there was no proof that Washoe intended the two signs to be taken together as a "bird that inhabits water"—it could have meant "a bird and some water," or even just "bird" and "water."

Herbert Terrace and his colleagues severely set back the idea of teaching apes language—research funds to do this sort of work became very difficult to get, and journals were reluctant to publish the research that was done. However, Terrace himself didn't escape criticism. Some experts have argued that Nim was a disturbed and insecure animal, one which could never have been expected to perform very well anyway. They claim that the conditions under which Nim was trained were so unpleasant (six hours of training a day in a plain white room) and devoid of stimulation that it is no wonder the chimp was unable to come up with anything really startling in his signing. There have also been arguments that by not accepting answers to "what" or "where" questions for fear that they would simply be imitative, Terrace wasn't admitting the very utterances that children's language abilities are often measured by: how they answer these sorts of questions.

One Terrace critic, Philip Lieberman (of Neanderthal fame) comes close to calling Terrace a liar over the "water bird" story. Why, Lieberman has written, did Terrace refer only to that example to dismiss the idea of creative signing, when there was already a record of other novel pairings of signs produced by other chimps, like "cry fruit" for "radish," or "drink fruit" for "watermelon": "It is difficult to see how Terrace could have been unaware of these data."[59] The scientist who had reported Washoe's use of the two signs for "water bird" added that the chimp used these signs to describe the swans even when they were out of the water! Exchanges like these are typical of the debate over chimps and language in the early 1980s. And that shouldn't come as a surprise: Terrace's criticisms really amounted to saying that other researchers had been sloppy, unintelligent or even unwittingly dishonest. It's no wonder they responded in kind.

But in a sense, whether Washoe or any other chimp combined signs in a novel way to describe something new is only part of the story, and in the long run, by no means the most important part. It can't be stressed too much that linguists deal primarily with the way words are arranged, and how meanings change as a result, not with the words themselves. And there are very few researchers who would insist that the chimps of the 1970s, Washoe, Sarah and others, had shown definitively that they were capable of that. (David Premack has admitted that there was nothing in his records of Sarah's selection of symbols that suggested she had any grasp of grammar or the structure of language.) But what do chimps have to do to satisfy anyone that they *are* capable of language in its fullest sense?

Here of course (do I have to say it again?) there's considerable disagreement, but Derek Bickerton, a linguist from the University of Hawaii (who will return with a vengeance in the next chapter), has suggested some rules. He agrees that chimps have already shown that they're capable of knowing that symbols aren't restricted to the particular example they're looking at—they know for instance, that "banana" means all the fruit of that description, not just the one on the table. They also realize that a man isn't a banana. But, he says, they should be able to use the word banana reliably when there isn't one in front of them, and more important, they have to demonstrate they can learn other kinds of words, like articles and conjunctions, because without those they can't harness the real power of language. Bickerton says it's not enough that a chimpanzee proves she knows the difference between Roger tickles Lucy and Lucy tickles Roger, although that's important. They also must learn that even when the words are in the same order, you can have different meanings: "Lucy tickled Roger and Lucy was tickled by Roger." And you can have the same meaning with different orders: "It was Roger that tickled Lucy" and "It was Lucy that Roger tickled." Language allows you to say the same thing in different ways. And while you're thinking about how tricky those ideas would be to get across, imagine the problems of complying with one of Bickerton's other requirements, that of imbedding a clause in the middle of a sentence: "Do the people *who are in the lab* eat bananas?"

So far I've made ape-language research sound as though it was exciting in the sixties and seventies, but a dead issue by the eighties. But that's not the case. It looks as if there's a whole new round to be fought, with the big difference being one new animal: a pygmy chimp named Kanzi. If any ape can change minds about the chimpanzee's language ability, it's this one.*

Kanzi was born in captivity in October 1980; he is a pygmy chimpanzee, or what's properly called a bonobo. They are native to Zaire, and are a different species from the common chimpanzees, the animals made famous by the work of Dr Jane Goodall, and the ones that have been involved in all the language experiments to date. The bonobos are a species in real danger of extinction: they might only last a couple of decades in the jungles of Zaire, and there are now too few in captivity to guarantee survival. They are much like the more common chimpanzee, except that they are closer to humans in their social behaviour, apparently using many facial expressions and gestures when communicating, and copulating face to face. However, they are not known to use tools in the wild, as common chimps do. When Kanzi was two

---

* Kanzi is apparently bright in many ways. He has learned to make his own stone tools to cut strings and slit open plastic covers to get at food, something he never would have had to do in the wild. Experiments are now under way to see if he can teach other chimpanzees to do the same thing, and also to see if Kanzi will learn to leave tool kits at locations where he has found food before, rather than hauling the tools around with him or having to return to where he keeps them every time he discovers food.

and a half he was separated briefly from his mother (who had already begun her own language training) and he suddenly, without any coaxing at all, began to use her board and the symbols on it to request food and activities and announce what he was about to do.[60] In *one day* he showed that he had learned signs his mother had failed to learn. His trainers, led by Dr Sue Savage-Rumbaugh, decided that from that point on Kanzi should be trained to use symbols, but that his training would reflect the casual, spontaneous learning he had already demonstrated. Kanzi has never been required to use symbols to get anything—if he does use them it is because he has seen someone else using them, in much the same way (it's thought) a child learns to speak.

Kanzi is quite different from all other chimpanzees that have been taught to use symbols to express their thoughts. For one thing, he understands spoken English. Of course, so did Fellow the dog, but other chimpanzees have not, and Kanzi can now demonstrate he understands more than two hundred English words by hearing them and then pointing to the appropriate symbol depicted on a board. (He actually chooses the correct sign from a choice of three symbols, and the trainer with him can't influence Kanzi's choice because she can't hear the word—it's the chimp language version of a "blind" experiment.)

Kanzi's mother cannot understand spoken words, but his sister can, suggesting that this skill has to be taught to chimpanzees, or at least bonobos, when they are young. Kanzi's trainers have even tested him with words produced by a speech synthesizer, one that produces a sound for every letter of the alphabet and comes out with a very weird, flat, clipped montonous kind of speech, only two-thirds of which is understandable by adult humans. Kanzi understands about two-thirds of it as well, meaning that the emotional content, unintentional stresses on words and any of the other cues that might have tipped him to the meaning of words spoken by his trainers cannot explain his understanding of speech. In fact, Kanzi understood 104 out of 150 synthesizer words: a four-year-old child got only 33. However, those are only words, and being able to translate them into symbols doesn't make Kanzi a linguist.

But he apparently understands sentences too. In one situation, Kanzi was playing with a ball near the river, and his trainer said, "Are you going to throw the ball into the river?" Kanzi, who had never done that, turned and threw the ball into the river. It could be argued that he didn't understand the word ball, that it just happened to be the object he already had in his hand, and all he might have grasped was "throw" and "river." Even so, that's not bad. He also understands short sentences like "Take the sour cream to the fridge," and "Put the straw in the bin." Again you can't use the fact that Kanzi then does the right thing to prove he understands the meaning of the word order, because it would be difficult to put the fridge in the sour cream, but again at the very least it shows that Kanzi is progressing fast.

Dr Sue Savage-Rumbaugh has been working with Kanzi since he first started to use symbols, and she feels that the most important task is to make sure he understands what's being said and what's expected of him. In the jargon, he needs to be capable of "multisymbol comprehension" before he's likely to produce "meaningful multi-symbol utterances," and maybe that has been the problem up till now. If the best a chimp can do in his longest statement is "give orange me give eat orange me eat orange give me eat orange give me you," as was the case with Herbert Terrace's Nim, that's a hint that the animal doesn't know what's going on. After all, a human can come out with lots of words without knowing what they mean! It would be a little like Victor, the wild child, saying "*lait*," but not really knowing that was the word for "milk."

Many scientists would agree that Kanzi has demonstrated a surprising understanding of spoken English. There is also evidence that he can comprehend grammatically complicated commands, as long as they're precise. So if there's an orange sitting in front of Kanzi, and he's told, "Go to the colony room and get the orange," he hesitates (is he thinking, "this orange?"). But if the sentence is rearranged: "Get the orange that's in the colony room," he has no trouble, even though there's that complicated (for a chimp) phrase in the middle, "that's in the." In fact at age eight Kanzi was better at understanding such sentences than a two-year-old girl named Alia who was being asked the same sorts of questions. (On the other hand, she was better at retrieving two objects: "Can you give so-and-so the peas and the sweet potatoes?")

But beyond this it gets more difficult—is Kanzi capable of putting together symbols in ways that would indicate he understands the importance of the order of words, and the differences in meaning that result when words, or symbols, are changed around? Savage-Rumbaugh and her colleague Patricia Marks Greenfield are convinced that at least at a simple level, he does. So for instance, when his mother, Matata, was grabbed by a trainer, he signed "Grab Matata." But when Matata bit someone, he changed the order to read, "Matata bite." And surprisingly, he is even said to be capable of making up new grammatical rules, ones that he's never been exposed to. An example is that when Kanzi wants two actions to take place, like "chase" and "hide," he always signs the first action first. And it shouldn't be forgotten that children learn to understand first and only then start to produce sentences, and Kanzi might well be the same.

However, even a brilliant performance by Kanzi is going to be treated with caution by the skeptics, and there has already been some doubt cast on exactly what the symbols on the board (which for the most part are stylized geometric figures, like a star, a pitchfork or a wavy line) mean to Kanzi. McGill University's Laura Pettito and Mark Seidenberg have argued that because Kanzi switches from one meaning to another for a given symbol, depending on the context, the symbols cannot mean the same thing to him as a word means to a child.[61] For instance, Kanzi will use "juice" to refer to the "drink," the place where he gets the drink, or the act of going to that place. But when tested for his vocabulary, he links the symbol "juice" with the picture of a glass of juice. These critics use this evidence to claim that Kanzi just uses the symbol as a means of solving different problems in different circumstances and has no idea that it means "juice" all the time. This sounds like a tricky argument, because children do what appears to be the same sort of thing, like pointing to the chair and saying, "Daddy." But Seidenberg and Petitto say that children rarely use a word for two different *kinds* of things, like using "table" to mean both the thing in the kitchen and breakfast, whereas Kanzi does.

It will be difficult to convince skeptics. Bertrand Russell once said, "I'd be prepared to accept that an ape can speak when someone presents for my consideration a specimen that could fathom the meaning of a sentence such as 'My father was poor but honest.'" Kanzi's linguistic prowess certainly isn't up to those standards. And really, he hasn't exactly demonstrated he understands the complexities that can be generated by changing orders in the several ways mentioned by Derek Bickerton. But he is probably more capable than the other chimps that came before him, and his trainers are being very careful to eliminate the sorts of weaknesses pointed out in previous studies. In fact, Sue Savage-Rumbaugh participated in some of the early work on chimpanzees and became disillusioned because she felt that the claims of success with language were exaggerated. Even if apes are capable of learning language, and Kanzi is the best current bet to reveal it, Sue Savage-Rumbaugh is a realist: she warns that given that chimps have brains only a third the size of ours, it is inevitable that they will be incapable of some aspects of language that we do routinely.

The motivation for doing this research is not to prove that there's nothing unique about humans, but to try to understand better how language might have begun. It's clear now that some monkeys, like the vervets of the African savannah, use different calls for different threats: their "eagle" call is different from the "snake" call, and prompts a different reaction (looking up rather than down). But chimpanzees engage in very little vocal communication of any complexity (although the bonobos haven't been studied very well in this regard in the jungle). Why would they possess the ability to use language if they don't use it in the wild? Evolution should only create abilities that enhance survival, and if you don't use language, how is it helping your survival?

This is a crucial issue, but everywhere you look in modern language research there are questions of equal importance, and there's really no hope that all of them will be answered to the satisfaction of everyone involved—that would be both impossible and boring. Sometimes the best way to play the game is to ask the most interesting questions, regardless of the answers that come out. You'll learn something important, even if you can't predict what that will be. In this case, trying to teach a chimp language may end up telling us almost nothing about language, but something unexpected about social behaviour or evolution or thinking. But think of the possibilities: if Kanzi appears to understand the meanings of symbols, let's get him under a positron emission tomography machine, and see what parts of his brain light up when he sees "banana"! We're bound to learn something.

18

<<<   When Children Invent
a Language

Between 1500 and 1900, England, France, the
Netherlands, Portugal and Spain inadvertently carried out a massive experiment in linguistics, one
that could eventually tie together a set of apparently disparate questions about language learning: do
apes really have the capacity to learn language; at
what point—and how—do children make the leap
to from simple one-word statements to true language; and what accounts for people like Genie,
who seem incapable of learning language once
they are past a critical age?

When they were at their peak, the colonial pow-
ers turned many of the isolated tropical islands
they'd conquered into huge farms, often devoted
to a single crop. They imported cheap human
labour to plant and harvest the crops from which
they then profited. But it's not the economic
exploitation that attracts the interest of linguists—
it's the languages that workers who were brought

together from many different countries were forced to speak under these circumstances. Many of the ideas in this chapter originated with linguist Derek Bickerton, who has studied the Hawaiian history of imported labour closely. Hawaii is a good example because there are specific dates available for the events there.[62] In 1876 US tariff laws were changed to allow the free importation of Hawaiian sugar, and that opened up the sugar cane industry on the islands. Immediately, Filipinos, Chinese, Japanese, Koreans, Puerto Ricans and others were shipped to Hawaii to work the sugar cane crop. By 1900, these foreign workers outnumbered speakers of English and Hawaiian by two to one. And how did they communicate with each other? They obviously couldn't use their native languages, and there weren't enough colonials around to teach them English (often in these island agricultural economies the workers outnumbered the owners thirty to one). Even if there had been, differences in social class would have made the spread of the colonial language difficult. So workers, wherever they were, made their own language: pidgin. A pidgin language is a form of what's already spoken there—in the case of Hawaii, English was the common denominator, so pidgin English became the language of the workers.

Pidgin English, or pidgin anything, is a greatly simplified form of talk. It contains lots of nouns and names for things, but very few of the words that connect sentences, introduce clauses, any of the mortar for the bricks—in that sense, broken

English isn't a bad description. (Or broken French, German or Thai: nonetheless pidgin is a lot more sophisticated than the crude attempts at local languages most tourists achieve.) Even the order of words is inconsistent—it doesn't have the rules for order that characterize any fully developed language. It takes many different forms, depending on the original language of the speaker: verbs, for instance, will shift around, depending on whose pidgin you're listening to. But it serves the purpose—most of the workers were past the age when it would be easy to learn a new language, and there really wasn't an opportunity to be consistently exposed to such a language anyway, so they fell back on pidgin. It got the job done in Hawaii and on many other islands, even though expressing complicated ideas in pidgin is sometimes difficult:

(Pidgin) "Some time good road get, sometime, all same bend get, enguru (angle) get, no? All kind same. All same human life, all same."

(English) "Sometimes there's a good road, sometimes there's like bends, corners, right? Everything's like that. Human life is just like that."

Here's another example—it's written phonetically and should be sounded out just as it appears:

"Aena tu macha churen, samawl churen, haus mani pei."

(English) "And too much children, small children, and I had to pay the rent.

But what happened next in Hawaii (and other places) is what's really exciting. Foreign workers married and had children. Some of these children would have grown up in households in which Chinese or Japanese was being spoken (if both parents were the same nationality) but the children would be under strong peer pressure to speak the language everyone else was speaking. Much more commonly the parents came from different ethnic backgrounds, and so pidgin was spoken in the house. Yet these children ended up speaking, not pidgin, but a different language altogether: Hawaiian Creole. This new language was already fully established in Hawaii by 1920.

Creole English is not at all like pidgin. Pidgin is super-simplified, a mix of concrete words strung together without much regard for rules, a language of necessity. Creole, on the other hand, has all the features of a true language: grammatical rules, constraints on word order, the rules that dictate which word modifies which, the things that make any language versatile and powerful. In English, you might say,

"If I had a car, I would go home."

A creole speaker would say, "If I bin get car, I go drive home." "Bin" is a parallel to "had," and "go" is used to express something conditional, or what the linguists call "irreal." We use "would." Not only does this example show that creole has its own rules, but it's clear that those rules differ from English, and therefore, according to Derek Bickerton, make it unlikely that Hawaiian Creole was adapted from English.

Look at how the word order changes in these sentences, all of which express the idea that

different people have different beliefs:
  "Some guys they get different belief."
  "They get different belief, some guys."
  "Different belief some guys they get."
Each different order for the words in those sentences changes the emphasis, and the words aren't just being moved around randomly: "different belief" creeps towards the front of the sentence while "some guys" gradually gets bumped to the back. All these versions of the sentence are grammatical in creole, but "Some guys, different belief they get" or "They get, some guys, different belief" would not be. Once you've seen a few examples like this you realize that creole languages, often dismissed as primitive and crude, are nothing of the kind—they might sound that way at first hearing because many slang words become incorporated into a creole vocabulary, but it pays to look beyond the words to the way they're put together.[63]

The question is, where did Hawaiian Creole come from? There were too many versions of pidgin spoken to be able to blend them into one uniform creole, and neither English nor any of the first languages of the immigrants have left their stamp on it either. As Derek Bickerton has pointed out, even if it had been possible to select a little from this language and a little from that, how could the whole population have agreed on what to take from each language to make a single creole? None of the simple explanations work: in one generation the children of pidgin-speaking adults in Hawaii created a whole new language complete with consistent and sensible rules. It seems to be a feat that defies any of the standard explanations for how children learn language.

That's amazing enough, but it's not the end of the story, because Hawaii is just one example of this process. Creole languages have developed in many other parts of the world where the circumstances were roughly the same, and those creole languages also bear no resemblance to the languages the children might have heard around them. But they do bear one resemblance: to each other! They all exhibit features not shared either by the colonial language where they arose, or by the original languages of the workers who had immigrated. For instance, in Hawaiian Creole, there is a distinction made between setting out to do something and accomplishing it or not. An English sentence like "I went to Ottawa to see the Prime Minister" wouldn't work in creole. You would have to indicate whether you actually got in to see the PM "Bin go Ottawa go see Brian," or not "Bin go Ottawa for see Brian." The startling thing is that creoles in Jamaica and Mauritius (off the east coast of Africa) demand the same distinction. This is not something that Derek Bickerton discovered himself—the similarities among creoles worldwide has been known for decades. The problem has been to explain it.

One suggestion has been that all creoles are descended from one that was derived from Portuguese as early as the 1500s, and was then gradually spread around the world wherever

Portuguese sailors went. The theory goes on that the skeleton of this early creole remained constant, even though the vocabulary changed to suit local circumstances. But Bickerton and his colleagues, by making an intensive study of the Hawaiian example, have been able to eliminate that possibility. Their evidence shows that Hawaiian Creole is not at all like Portuguese, and that it originated in Hawaii. The only conclusion you can come to is that this language was invented by the children of immigrants to Hawaii in the late nineteenth and early twentieth centuries, and presumably other creoles (although perhaps not *all* others) arose the same way.

If all of this is true, the only way to explain the detailed structure of Hawaiian Creole and the resemblance of that structure to other creoles is to say that somehow children everywhere, if more or less left to their own devices, will make up the same kind of language. They must be born with a built-in plan for creating a language, and Derek Bickerton thinks that this plan—as long as there are no other influences—will create a creole language. According to this theory, creole is the fundamental human language.

This is startling enough, but he goes further. He thinks that the one- and two-word talk of children under two, the pidgin languages which adults use if they are forced to, and the earliest languages spoken by our ancient human ancestors are all the same: they are not-quite-languages (he calls them "protolanguages") characterized by a lack of rules and the absence of the little words that help create the structure of true language. And, in Bickerton's opinion, you can add apes to that group too. He admits that children use some rules to determine the order of words even in their two-word statements, but he's not convinced this represents an early version of the adult use of word order. Some ape-language researchers have compared the kinds of word sequences that apes sign to the spoken language of a two-year-old and point out that they look the same. Bickerton agrees, but by doing so gives no comfort to the ape enthusiasts, because he thinks neither the apes nor the children are using real language!

The argument is that children aren't *yet* capable of true language (possibly because the brain hasn't matured), apes will *never* be capable, pidgin speakers are forced to revert to this kind of language just to communicate, and our ancestors hadn't yet evolved the linguistic ability to get beyond this stage. Genie would be a rare example of an adult who, because she was prevented from learning language during the critical period, was doomed to remain in the pre-linguistic state. In fact Bickerton makes a point of describing Genie not as a child who had failed to acquire a full version of human language, but a child who "has acquired something *other than full human language*."

It's a fantastic concept, exciting because it ties together so many ideas of how language appears— in fact, it sounds so good that you suspect it must somehow be wrong! Obviously some of these claims are impossible to test, like the idea that ancient hominids spoke the equivalent of a creole language. We also can't say that apes will *never* be able to use language in its fullest sense. But what about children—if it's true that they are all born with a blueprint for a creole language, shouldn't there be some evidence for that?

Noam Chomsky has suggested that children have, in addition to their language organ or blueprint, a set of switches that enable a child in any culture to tune into the language being spoken around him. If you had been born in Italy instead of Canada, or vice versa, different switches would (somehow) have been thrown so you could assimilate the structure of the other language. Derek Bickerton thinks that in the absence of any such language, no switches are thrown, and you end up speaking creole. And that's not all—he argues that there are examples from English that suggest that children sometimes have a tough time suppressing this innate tendency to speak creole. One example he gives is the difficulty children have with negatives.

Linguists have shown that children generally learn negatives in a straightforward way: at first they just attach the word "no" to the beginning of an otherwise normal sentence. The "no" can also occasionally appear at the end of the sentence, but never in the middle. Then they progress to a second stage in which the words "no," "not," "can't" and "don't" are used, and these words are now free to move into the sentence, right after the subject and before the verb—they must be before the verb. At this stage children seem not to be aware that "can't" and "don't" are contractions of "can," "do" and "not." And one thing they never do is put "can't" at the beginning of a sentence. Finally (and there is no set timetable for this), they realize that "can't" can be split, and they start coming out with sentences like, "I did not caught it." It takes a little longer to learn that the "did" makes it unnecessary to use "caught." This sequence of steps is used by many children (although not all—one little girl named Jennifer was observed expressing negatives simply by raising the pitch of her voice!).

This is not to suggest this happens easily. One of the commonest problems is the tendency children have to hang on to double negatives. In one session observed by linguist David McNeill, a four-year-old persisted in saying, "Nobody don't like me." His mother corrected him, saying, "Nobody likes me." Again and again it happened. Finally after the eighth repetition, the boy finally said in exasperation, "Nobody don't like**s** me."

Creole languages are full of double negatives: "Non dag na bait non kyat" in Guyanese Creole ("No dog did not bite no cat") is typical. Are children who have trouble ridding their English of double negatives just hanging on to their creole language blueprint a little too long? As the other side of that coin, English-speaking children learn the "ing" ending early and usually use it properly right from the beginning: they hardly ever say, "I liking," or "I wanting." Those sorts of combinations aren't allowed in creole languages either.

Derek Bickerton has provided a tantalizing explanation for language learning that ties many different kinds of speech together. It requires two stages in learning a language, and in fact two kinds of language: the first one, the "protolanguage," is the one that presumably appeared first in our evolution, and it's also what children first speak. (For this to be true, children would have to switch abruptly from proto to true language, a kind of caterpillar to butterfly transition, and there are many linguists who don't believe there's sufficient evidence that this happens. If they switched gradually, there presumably would exist all kinds of intermediate languages, and that is not the case.) Protolanguage would also be what adults resort to when thrown into situations in which their own language can't be used. It might be the kind of simple assembling of symbols or signs that chimpanzees have shown they can do. It's even been suggested that under the right circumstances, anybody can revert to using this simple but ancient form of communication. If you're extremely tired or drunk or ill, you may find yourself speaking in three- or four-word phrases and abandoning the rules of sentence structure that you've been using since you were four or five years old. It's in those inarticulate moments that you might be reliving, not just your own prelinguistic past, but that of our entire species.

19

<<< Conversation Pieces

Hearing Strange Voices

The single most amazing statistic I've encountered in writing this book came out of a survey of college students in the early 1980s that established, astonishingly, that seventy-one percent had experienced auditory hallucinations at one time or another.[64] Seventy-one percent! Thirty-nine percent reported hearing their own thoughts aloud, as in the case of a student taking a math exam who heard, "That one is wrong"; another heard her dead grandfather giving her advice as to what dress to wear to his funeral. Five percent even reported having conversations with those voices.

This claim—that nearly three out of four people have heard voices at one time or another in their lives—can't be dismissed easily, because earlier studies had reported the same thing, although the numbers weren't quite as high. You can only conclude that hearing voices is relatively common in the general population.* This comes as a shock to most because we're used to thinking that hearing voices is a sign of madness. It obviously isn't, and the fact that you don't have to be crazy to hear the occasional voice may make it easier to understand why some disturbed people hear them all the time.

Most of those college students who reported hearing voices had had it happen rarely, sometimes only once. But people with schizophrenia often have to endure voices talking to them constantly. Schizophrenia is a serious mental disorder that—contrary to popular belief—has nothing to do with having two separate minds in one brain or anything like that. The "split" in schizophrenia is between reality and the world in which the schizophrenic lives. The voices sometimes come out of nowhere, or occasionally develop out of a normal room sound, like the noise of a refrigerator; or may even come from something as incongruous as a pencil eraser. The schizophrenic may hear

---

* In a 1964 study seventy-eight secretaries were given the following instructions: "I want you to close your eyes and hear a phonograph record with words and music playing 'White Christmas.' Keep listening to the record until I tell you to stop." After thirty seconds the subjects were asked to give their impressions of what they had just experienced. Forty-nine percent reported that they had actually *heard* the record. There have been follow-up studies that have produced similar results, a strong suggestion that the right setting might make hearing things a lot easier.

himself being discussed ("What he doesn't know is that all these people are watching him ...") or maybe addressed directly by the voices, or can hear his own thoughts—even before he thinks them!

Schizophrenics' hallucinated voices are often abusive and derisory, providing a running commentary on what they're doing, telling them what they *should* be doing, or just dismissing the captive listener as worthless. The voice may belong to someone unknown, a deceased relative, or to God or the Virgin Mary.

Researchers have puzzled over the source of these voices for decades. Obviously they come from the schizophrenic's own thoughts, but how do those thoughts become voices, and how do those voices become attributed to someone else? There are many theories as to how this happens (schizophrenia is still a poorly understood condition), but one links the voices of schizophrenics to something that we all do, and might at the same time explain why so many non-psychotic people occasionally experience auditory hallucinations.

This theory argues that hallucinations are disturbances of a normal process called "inner speech." It's a little tricky to pin down exactly what inner speech is, but one of the best ways to begin to understand it is to start with exactly what you're doing as you read this sentence. You're speaking the words to yourself—a voice inside your head sounds the words as you go along. When you first learned to read you probably spoke

the words out loud, but as you became more proficient, you began to read silently. The example of
silent reading should give you an idea of the kind
of voice that's involved in inner speech, but inner
speech is much more than just inwardly speaking
words as you read them. Many psychologists have
suggested that inner speech is nothing less than
thought, claiming that as you think, you actually
hear—in your head—words that represent your
thoughts.

It seems hard to imagine that *all* thought would
parade through our brain as unspoken words
(what words would a painter or musician be using
as inner speech to describe a piece they were creating?). But once you start thinking about inner
speech, you'll probably find that much of your
thinking during the day *does* exist, at least for
moments, as words in your brain, whether you
eventually speak them or not.

Difficult as it is to study inner speech, there
have been attempts to describe it: it's said to be a
shorthand version of real speech (as one researcher
put it, a word in inner speech is "the mere skin of
a thought"), and it's very egocentric, not surprisingly, given that it's a monologue, with the speaker
and the audience being the same person. There
have even been experiments to try to bring inner
speech out into the light, and examine it.

One of these was an attempt to measure the
speed of inner speech.[65] A psychologist named
Rodney Korba presented volunteers with words
that had letters missing. They were to figure out, in

their heads, what the missing letters were, then say the completed word out loud. So for instance, the subjects saw the letters "_UIT_ASE." As soon as they figured out the missing letters, they would say "suitcase." A harder one was "_AR_A_E": here two possible answers were "garbage" or "yardage." As soon as the experimental subjects had uttered the target word, Korba had them write down all the words, letters, combinations of letters, instructions to themselves, or anything else that went on in their minds while they were trying to solve the puzzle. Then, as a second step, they were to explain fully the meaning of those bits of inner speech.

Dr Korba was able to come up with some numbers, including an estimate for the rate of inner speech, just by dividing the number of inner speech words (or thoughts or letters) that had flashed through the subjects' minds as they tried to solve the problem, by the time it took them to come up with the answer. He calculated that inner speech produced six "words" per second, each of which required more than ten words of normal speech to explain. That works out to a inner rate equivalent to four thousand spoken words every minute.

Now this *is* iffy: many of the people taking part in the experiment expressed dissatisfaction with their attempts to remember and record all the words, letters and so on that had appeared in their minds in the few seconds they took to solve these puzzles. It would be much better to be able to visualize inner speech directly as it goes on in the brain, using some sort of brain imaging device, without having to rely on people trying to describe what's going on in their own heads. But the trick would be knowing that the brain activity you might see was actually inner speech, and not some other unknown mental goings-on that have nothing to do with it.

There have been attempts to detect inner speech by trying to measure, not brain waves themselves, but activity in the muscles of the lip, tongue and throat that control speech. The rationale for doing this is the long-held suspicion that the sequence of events in inner speech is the same as that for talking out loud, except for the last step of actually producing the speech sounds. Only at this last second is inner speech curbed, so that even though we don't utter its words, we come pretty close. The first attempts to try to detect the silent traces of inner speech were, by today's standards, crude: researchers in the 1920s attached a suction cup to the tongue and in turn to a lever, to see if the lever moved when the person was thinking. That experiment failed—it really was too much to expect that the tongue would actually move—but it was on the right track. Once researchers took one step back from trying to see actual movement, and instead used instruments to detect electrical signals coming to the tongue and lips from the brain, the signals that would normally set them into the movements of speech, they started to get results.

The apparatus that detects these brain-to-muscle

signals is called the electromyograph, and studies using it have shown that the same muscles are activated when a person actually speaks as when they think the same sequence of words to themselves. There is also increased speech muscle activity when people are engaged in silent reading, memorizing and or even making up arguments in their head. This latter example refers to a study in which the experimental subjects were warned that they were going to hear opinions expressed on an audiotape that attacked their position on some issue that was important to them personally.[66] When they were told this, the electrical activity in their speech muscles increased. The lists of thoughts these same people reported having at that time suggested that this increased muscle activity was the outward sign of the brain marshalling arguments to counter opinions it was about to hear!

It's quite fantastic to contemplate that even as you're working your way through a complicated sequence of ideas in your head, you are sending messages to your speech muscles telling them to mouth those words. And that they don't, because something inhibits them at the last split-second.

Unfortunately in the study above where an attempt was made to measure the rate of inner speech, Rodney Korba wasn't able to correlate the recordings of signals on the electromyograph with the estimates by his problem-solvers of how many discrete words or pieces of inner speech they had produced. He virtually admitted that it would have been a big surprise if there *had* been a perfect correlation between bursts of electrical activity and "words" in the head. It must be more complicated than that.

At the same time as some researchers have been trying to detect inner speech in the favourite lab animal of psychologists, the undergraduate student, others have been studying the hallucinations of schizophrenics in the same way. Many believe that hallucinated voices are just inner speech gone wrong. (When I say just, I'm ignoring for the moment that the *content* of those hallucinations is very different from the content of inner speech in non-schizophrenics.) With the aid of an electromyograph, a series of experiments in the late 1940s and early 1950s established that auditory hallucinations were accompanied by electrical activity in the throat, lips and tongue. It began when the hallucinations began, and appeared in eighty-three percent of those having hallucinations, and only ten percent of those not. The voices that seem to the patient to be coming from God, or the shower head, were coming from their own brains.

A study in England in the early 1980s took this one bizarre step further.[67] Two psychologists, Paul Green and Martin Preston, had noticed that a fifty-one-year-old schizophrenic, although medicated, still laughed and talked to himself. He was also seen occasionally turning his head to one side as if listening, then moving his lower lip and whispering. He wasn't aware of the whispering, but was aware of a female voice that he called "Miss

Jones." When the psychologists attached two throat microphones to the patient, they found that his own whispers were actually the comments that he attributed to "Miss Jones." The situation became even stranger when Drs Green and Preston amplified and played the whispers back to the patient *as he was uttering them*. He then started to whisper louder, until eventually the whispers were as loud as his normal speech, and they could easily hear the conversation between him and Miss Jones! Miss Jones's voice was a little distorted and clearly different from the patient's, and it made comments he would never have made himself: "It's me. We're on tape." "He's a bit mental. Leave him alone. ..." "Mind your own business darling. I don't want him [the psychologist] to know what I was doing."

When the tape was replayed to the patient, he said he couldn't understand how Miss Jones's comments had been taped, because she was a "real and separate person" he had known for two years. He also denied that he talked to himself. When confronted with a segment of the tape containing his own normal voice alternating with the whispers, he said, "It's funny that she should speak to me and then it's my voice speaking." It was a fascinating though somewhat pathetic demonstration of the reality of auditory hallucinations. This case might be extreme—there must be many schizophrenics who hear their own inner speech as hallucinated voices without ever actually mouthing the words. Either way, the fact that these mysterious voices might just be misinterpretations of inner speech has prompted some suggestions that reading, singing or even humming would prevent hallucinations because those activities would occupy the speech muscles. In some cases this approach seems to have reduced the number of hallucinations substantially.

To put this all together, we all talk silently to ourselves: that's the process called "inner speech" which some psychologists have equated with nothing less than thinking. That there is a brain process that connects to speech is clear from the recordings of electrical activity in the muscles controlling speech, often at just the times a person is thinking or talking to himself. There's also evidence that the hallucinated voices of schizophrenics are inner speech run amok, and that many people without a detectable mental disorder experience auditory hallucinations too.

There are still some very important unanswered questions, one of which is why schizophrenics hear their own inner speech as the words of someone else. Ralph Hoffman of Yale University has suggested that because schizophrenics have disordered thoughts, with no logical progression in their ideas, they might "hear" their inner speech going off in some direction they didn't intend, and assume as a result that it could only be someone else's voice. Critics have questioned how disorganized or disordered thoughts and speech can possibly explain why apparently large numbers of "normal" people have heard voices. And that's the other puzzle: what are the factors that can make nearly three out of every four people hear voices at one time or another?

History is full of charismatic figures who were led to perform great deeds at least partly because they heard a voice—often the voice of God. The list includes St Paul, Augustine, Caesar, Mohammed, Moses, Alexander the Great and William Blake. Some of them may have been mentally disturbed, but were they all? Not likely.

A recent attempt was made to diagnose the woman who is perhaps the best known of all these historical figures who heard voices: Joan of Arc. The physician who studied her case, Dr Fred Henker, decided that whatever she was, she wasn't a schizophrenic.[68]

St Joan freely admitted both to hearing the voice of God, and to seeing visions of St Michael, St Catherine and St Margaret. She had heard these voices from the age of thirteen, and they had urged her to get involved in the battle against the occupying British. Until the last moments before she was burned at the stake Joan maintained that the voices she heard came from God.

When Dr Henker tried to diagnose Joan, he concluded that she didn't satisfy the modern criteria for schizophrenia. In today's context a village girl who had a dream of leading an army to defeat an invading force would seem deluded, and delusions *are* characteristic of schizophrenia. But Henker felt that Joan's religious fervour and grandiose ambitions weren't unusual for the early

1400s. In fact her reports of hearing voices and seeing visions weren't atypical either, and neither the
delusions nor the hallucinations made Charles VII
or her army hesitant to throw in their lot with her.
More important, she showed none of the disordered thought that is typical of schizophrenia: during her trial, Joan matched eloquence and
intelligence with the numerous judges she faced.
Nor did she show any signs of mental deteriora-
tion with time. An editorial in the *Southern
Journal of Medicine* accompanying Dr Henker's
discussion of Joan's symptoms made the simple
point that it should come as no surprise that it's
hard to diagnose someone like Joan of Arc using
modern medical criteria. She was a mystic, and
you can't explain mystics rationally.

So people with mental disorders, mystics, and a
fair number of people from the general population
hear voices. This still isn't anywhere near the number of people who *used* to hear voices, if you buy
the ideas of Julian Jaynes, a psychologist at
Princeton University. In his book *The Origin of
Consciousness in the Breakdown of the Bicameral
Mind,* Jaynes argues that up until fairly recently in
human history, *everyone* heard voices, and those
voices told people what to do. Nobody made their
own decisions to take action—they were simply
following the orders of their hallucinated voices.
And Jaynes has proposed a mechanism for this too:
he suggests that prior to about 1500 BC, the two
cerebral hemispheres were not in constant commu-

nication as they are today. They were literally two minds in the same head, except that the right hemisphere would give orders to the left in the form of auditory hallucinations—the left would then carry out those orders, which it thought had come as a voice from the gods. Somehow, in those days of separate hemispheres, people were not conscious of themselves as beings with an identity, a past and a future. They were "bicameral," two-in-one, aware only of the here and now.

If it sounds all too bizarre, take Jaynes's favourite example, Homer's *Iliad*. This epic poem comes down to us, Jaynes argues, from pre-conscious or bicameral times. He claims that there are almost no examples in the *Iliad* of anyone acting on his own free will, or making decisions of any kind that aren't dictated by the gods. They never sit down and decide what they should do. When Agamemnon steals Achilles' mistress, a god warns Achilles not to retaliate. Gods start the quarrels that cause the war, gods plan the strategy, a god leads the armies into battle, a god whispers to Helen, gods do everything. When Achilles reminds Agamemnon that he has stolen his mistress, Agamemnon replies, "Not I was the cause of this act, but Zeus ..." The *Iliad* is only one example: there are many others that can be interpreted as showing that people at that time needed their own auditory hallucinations to act. Eventually humans became conscious when the two hemispheres of the brain began to communicate directly with each other, and Julian Jaynes argues that occurred during a period of societal upheaval roughly three thousand five hundred years ago.

It's impossible to do justice to Jaynes's thesis in only a few lines, but it's obvious that there are parellels between people whose every waking moment was dominated by what they thought were the voices of gods, and schizophrenics today, many of whose lives are also dominated by godlike voices. In the *Iliad*, the heroes of the tale are urged to act by their gods. In the wards of mental institutions today, psychotic patients often hear what are called "command" hallucinations—they are told to commit suicide or homicide or to injure themselves or others. The likelihood that such patients will actually obey their voices depends to some extent on whether they know who's speaking to them—they're more likely to act if the voice is identifiable as that of a dead relative or of God.

Do those schizophrenics who hear command hallucinations represent a return to a pre-conscious, bicameral era of human history? Julian Jaynes is certain that they do, and he adds that the presence of auditory hallucinations in virtually every culture (some of which view hearing voices as a gift, not an illness) argues that our brains still retain a vestige of the old bicameral set-up, and that under appropriate circumstances—religious ecstacy, psychotic breakdown, hallucinogenic drugs or even something relatively trivial like the stress of writing a crucial math exam—we may step back in time and hear the voices of the gods.*

Speaking in Tongues

"Mitchma mitchmon mimini tchouainem mimatchineg masichinof mezavi patelki abresinad navette naven navette ..." This is Martian, as spoken by the Swiss medium Hélène Smith, (a.k.a. Catherine Elise Muller) during one of her seances in the 1890s in which she reported travelling to

---

* At this point theories begin to clash. In Chapter Eighteen I described Derek Bickerton's idea that there is a "protolanguage" that toddlers, speakers of pidgin, some chimpanzees, and people deprived of the chance to learn language use. This protolanguage is supposed to come from the right hemisphere. In fact Bickerton claims that this very simple form of talk is all that hemisphere is capable of. If that were true, in the old bicameral days, the gods would have spoken to our left hemispheres in the kind of words that under-twos use. Humans would have been hallucinating baby-talk! And the *Iliad* would then sound like this:

"Agamemnon you bad! No Achilles fight Agamemnon ..."

the red planet and conversing with the inhabitants (actually she spoke four related languages: Martian, Ultra-Martian, Uranian and Lunar).[69] In this particular session, she spoke for a few minutes, most of the words being incomprehensible, and then suddenly said, "Oh I have had enough of it; you say such words to me I will never be able to repeat them." Three years' worth of Hélène Smith's seances—forty in all—were studied by the French psychologist Thomas Flournoy; he recorded a total of 160 different Martian words that she used during that time, and analyzed how those words were put together.

Flournoy concluded that the Martian language was, in every sense except the vocabulary, identical to French: same grammatical rules, same sentence constructions, same rules of word order. Not only that—when Smith actually wrote out the Martian language using a weird set of hieroglyphs, it was possible in many cases to compare the Martian statements with their French equivalents word for word: "tu vois" (you see) became "de vechi"; "près de toi" (beside you) was, in Martian, "ten ti vi." Flournoy dismissed Hélène Smith's Martian as "naïve" and "counterfeit." He was right, but that sort of dismissal, which has been applied to phenomena like this again and again, misses one of the most important points: it's still amazing that she could produce so much unusual talk so consistently over such a long period of time. And that is still not easy to explain.

Hélène Smith's reports from Mars actually were

of two different kinds: the first words of Martian that she spoke came out so rapidly they couldn't be written down, and she was apparently completely unaware of what she had said. It was only after she had been quizzed on the meaning of some of the most common words that she began to use specific words over and over, and at the same time translate what she was conveying from the Martians—all of this without any evidence of being consciously aware of what she was doing. Some experts who have looked at this case think that all of Hélène Smith's "Martian" was actually *glossolalia*, or speaking in tongues, and the initial and unexpected outpouring was the moment when this phenomenon first struck Hélène Smith, probably to her complete surprise.

Speaking in tongues describes the experience people have when they start speaking what sounds like some foreign language, but not any language the speaker knows. It happens most often in a religious setting, in which someone begins to feel as if he is in contact with God or the Holy Spirit (at least in the North American Christian churches in which speaking in tongues is practised) and unearthly speech wells up out of him. People who experience it seem not to be in control of the sounds they make. Believers think that the sounds represent the words of the Holy Spirit, speaking through them, although there's a more moderate interpretation that argues that the words are indeed the person's own, although they are *inspired* by God. Skeptics think the whole thing is just a put-on. But there are linguists and anthropologists who have studied tongue-speaking in some detail, and they find it more interesting, but in some ways less strange, than you might think.

Speaking in tongues has been practised since the beginning of Christianity. It appears in the Bible in Acts 2, when the disciples are gathered together in Jerusalem, and suddenly begin to speak in a mix of foreign languages; pilgrims gather around and are astonished to hear their own languages being spoken, everything from Phrygian and Parthian to Arabic. This story notwithstanding, speaking in tongues has always been viewed with suspicion by most Christian denominations. In North America, speaking in tongues began to experience a revival in the 1950s in what's called the charismatic movement, especially in the Pentecostal church, but this is by no means the only Christian church in which it is practised—in North America alone there are probably tens of thousands of people who speak in tongues, and there are many times that number all over the world. Those who practise it in North America may speak in tongues several times every day!

Here's a typical example of how it happens: a person, man or woman, usually belongs to a church in which speaking in tongues is commonly heard, and is viewed as a desirable accompaniment to baptism. This person may or may not have been trying to speak in tongues for some time, but one day it happens: often in the midst of praying, she is overtaken by an overwhelming feeling, opens her mouth, and out comes a flood of talk in a language she has never heard before, and does not understand. Most of the time such a person had no idea what her tongue-speaking was going to sound like. It's not surprising, given the circumstances, that this person would report feeling as if the Holy Spirit had taken over her power to speak, and the words—if indeed they are words—had come from Him. And what are these words like?

"kupoy shandré filé sundrukuma shandré lasa hoya taki. fozhon shetireloso kumo shandré palaso shantré kamoyentri. sozhandri kaga sombo poyentre lapatsombo koyshantrala so."

That's an example of speaking in tongues recorded by Professor William Samarin, a man who has taken a keen interest in the linguistic character of this kind of speech. The speaker was a Reverend d'Esprit who worked extensively with Samarin. You look at that passage, and it looks like some sort of language that you've never seen before. But Samarin argues that in fact it is no language at all, because it doesn't have any of the features that languages have. There are no rules determining word order, grammar or how clauses can be stuck into the middle of sentences, no sounds that would indicate the future (like "will"), or pronouns, or plurals, nothing. The sounds just flow, on and on. This is not to say there isn't a pattern, and in fact it would be more obvious if you heard the above passage than you can tell just from reading it. But it is a pattern of tone, rhythm, and rising and falling pitch: nothing to do with the words themselves, or how they are organized into what seem to be phrases or even sentences.

In fact, Samarin pointed out that the way he transcribed the above tongue-speech was completely arbitrary. He could have written it as "ku poyshan dréfi lésundru" and on from there instead of "kupoy shandré filé sundrukuma," but he made a judgement from the lilt of the rhythm and the intonation that the breaks between sounds should appear as they do in the original transcription. The point is that there is no other information that would suggest that the speech is broken down into units like words. Even tongue-speakers themselves, upon hearing a tape of their own voices from a few hours before, often can't repeat what they said.

That's not the only evidence that this apparently miraculous speech isn't a unique language, or even a language at all. For one thing, it's peppered with the sounds that appear in the speaker's native language, like this example making liberal use of "et cetera":

"Etce ce Tera. Lute te turo scente.

Inke Runo tere. Scete inte telee turo."

And of course Hélène Smith's "Martian" was really a sort of garbled French, and often the most common sounds in the speaker's native language appear even more often in the tongue-speech.* Yet

---

* As far as I know, there are no reports of auditory hallucinations in which the voices heard were speaking

most of the people who practise it believe they are speaking some language that they're not familiar with, certainly a foreign one, perhaps an ancient one. And let's face it: it's always possible to argue that because the words or feelings are those transmitted by the Holy Spirit, it's fruitless to try to apply the naïve and limited analysis of linguists to tongue-speech. Divine is divine, and beyond analysis and critique.

To add to the mystery, there have been many reports of a closely related phenomenon, technically called *xenoglossia*, which is supposed to be the speaking of real languages by people who are somehow inspired to do so—they have to be, because they have no knowledge of the language in question. So there's the story of a truck driver in Seattle who broke out spontaneously in Mandarin, and an Irishman in Texas who prayed in perfect Hebrew. In Gary, Indiana, Easter Sunday 1950, a member of the congregation stood up and spoke in tongues, and a group of Italian parishioners were stunned: they knew this man well, and were perfectly aware that he knew no Italian, yet he had just spoken Italian worthy—they said—of a university graduate. (Interestingly, it's usually people other than the speaker who are able to identify the

---

in tongues. That makes sense if tongue-speech isn't real language—it could suggest that the mental processes that lead to hallucinated voice wouldn't have access to something that's not language.

language.) Unfortunately most of these stories are second- or third-hand, and to date there's no recording of anyone speaking a language under extraordinary circumstances, followed by a demonstration that he or she is incapable of doing so normally.* Some of the more fervent believers, especially earlier this century, believed that missionaries had no need of learning the language of the country to which they were being assigned: they could simply speak the local language in tongues when they got there, and of course the

---

* With one exception. There is a case of a Jewish housewife who was raised in Philadelphia by parents who had emigrated from Russia before she was born. When she was in a hypnotic trance, she suddenly started to speak Swedish in a deep male voice and use the name Jenson Jacoby. At least one Swedish speaker heard her talking and confirmed that she was speaking proper Swedish (something that *never* happens when tongue-speakers who think they're speaking some African dialect are actually confronted with people who know it) mixed with some Norwegian and Danish. She had had no contact with Swedish, and even scored lower than average on a standard test for language-learning aptitude. When she wasn't living the Jacoby personality, she didn't understand a word of Swedish. I have never seen this particular example debunked. (I. Stevenson, *Xenoglossy: A Review and Report of a Case*, Charlotteville: University Press of Virginia, 1974)

people would understand them. Some apparently did so, although there's no record of the reaction they received.

The strangest thing about speaking in tongues is that it seems so bizarre and other-worldly, and yet the closer researchers look at it, the more ordinary it becomes. Because it often happens in a church setting, especially one of the so-called charismatic churches, you might have in your mind an impression of people falling down in a swoon, then suddenly spewing out these strange utterances, all the while apparently completely possessed. It is true that speaking in tongues can appear in exactly such a fashion, but these days it may happen in rather less exciting circumstances. The following is a description by a man who suddenly started to speak in tongues one night when he was all by himself:

"But on this night I was completely relaxed in my favourite place to relax (the bathtub) and was quietly praying and praising God in English when suddenly I realized I was not speaking English any more but a language unknown to me."

And this man is not alone. Nearly a quarter of people surveyed say that they started to speak in tongues when they were alone. Some people who already have the ability have reported doing it in the most unusual places, like when they're driving their truck, or test-piloting airplanes! This would suggest that they're not exactly in a trance or semi-conscious, and in fact many of the descriptions of tongue-speaking prove that people can do it and remain completely aware and alert at the same time. One person experiencing it for the first time even tried to analyze the words:

"All the while I was praising God in a marvellous language that I had never known. In my school days I had studied Latin, French, German and Spanish—but it was none of these."

It doesn't usually come unbidden—most people who speak in tongues have wanted to do so for some time, and have viewed it as an essential part of giving oneself up to God. It's commonly said that the acceptance of God is the important step, and the tongue-speaking will just come along with it. But some have tried to encourage it nonetheless, even murmuring nonsense syllables while they pray, or spending time with, and getting advice from, someone who's experienced. That's the other thing: once you are able to speak in tongues, you can work on it and get better. Some accomplished speakers have admitted being worried about repetition in their utterances, that their vocabulary is too restricted, and they work on putting more variety into it, more sounds and better rhythm. It would be hard to argue that you could somehow improve on the words of God; those who practise their speaking in tongues must be among those who believe that the words are indeed their own, however inspired they are. Some get so good at it that it appears to be effortless (one person was even reported to be able to tongue-speak while reading), and it begins somehow to sound more and more like an esoteric form of jogging or meditation than a conduit to the deity.

I'm not trying to argue that speaking in tongues is totally meaningless: it can have profound effects on both those who perform it and the audience— it's just that these owe nothing to the so-called words. William Samarin and others have argued that although there is no linguistic content in tongue-speaking, there is emotion. An utterance can be joyful or anxious, and that will be conveyed by the tone of voice and the rhythm, not the actual sounds. Listeners will understand at least the feelings being expressed. In fact there seems to be no importance attached to the order of the sounds: the fifth sentence could be the tenth and vice versa. It's the beat and the melody that count, not the lyrics. And yet there is something conveyed, and both the fact that there *is* a message and the claim that it's not carried by the words are borne out by the attempts made to interpret what tongue-speakers have said.

Interpretation in this case is not translation; there is nothing to translate. It is instead a running commentary, or an explanation of what the tongue-speech means, and without this interpretation much of tongue-speaking would remain incomprehensible. Interpretation is given by a speech that brings out the spirituality of the message, usually in Biblical language, with lots of thees and thous, without being a word-for-word version of what was said. That the two are not the same is made clear by the example of one episode of tongue-speaking that was transcribed in eight lines, while the interpretation was forty-three!

Some people are never able to do it, and given that they are usually active in a church in which tongue-speaking is not only accepted, but welcomed as a sign of having received the Holy Spirit, this failure can be depressing. It is also a sign that however ordinary some of the testimony about speaking in tongues makes it appear, there is much that is yet to be learned about it. Why is it that some people can do it and others can't? Does it have to do with giving up some sort of mental control over yourself, and allowing these sounds just to come out? That might explain why some who are trying so hard to achieve it cannot.

Traditionally psychologists and psychiatrists have viewed tongue-speaking as a sign of mental disturbance. One idea was that the people who do it are retarded or illiterate, or a combination of both, so that when driven by the excitement of the moment and religious fervour, and seized with the desire to say something but without the intellect to say it, they lose control and start speaking in tongues. Today this theory wouldn't seem to make much sense: people who speak in tongues are not mentally disturbed. Mob hysteria (which doesn't apply to the guy in the bathtub), mass hypnosis (likewise) or just a complete lack of rational control have all been suggested too. The problem is that there is absolutely no evidence of any mental abnormality of any kind that's been found in people who speak in tongues. They are normal people. But surely they can't be—somehow when they *are* speaking in tongues something strange must be happening to them?

Apparently not. A wide variety of physiological measurements have been taken simultaneously of people speaking and not speaking in tongues, and there are no differences between the two groups. This really should come as no great surprise: you'd hope that someone who's driving a truck while speaking in tongues is not in some sort of altered state of consciousness. To my knowledge no sophisticated brain-scanning techniques have been used that might illustrate which areas of the brain are active when people speak in tongues, and whether these are the same areas that light up when they are speaking normally. Those would be very interesting, because theoretically these people wouldn't be having to retrieve the words of any sort, or assemble them into sensible phrases and sentences when they speak in tongues. The question is, would that difference be visible in positron emission tomography? To date, this experiment hasn't been done.

There are some hints of long-term effects on the person who is a successful tongue-speaker. There have been at least two well-done studies that show that tongue-speakers tend less towards depression than non-speakers. Of course, this may have much more to do with the attainment of higher spirituality, and relatively little to do with any direct effects of tongue-speaking on the brain.

And that's just about where it stands: tongue-speaking is on the surface an extremely strange, even bewildering behaviour, yet the people who do it are just like everyone else. You might even be able to learn to do it yourself.

Foreign Accent Syndrome

In the world of language unusual individuals turn up all the time: sometimes they have surprising language abilities, like the young man in England who, although not capable of taking care of himself on a daily basis, is nonetheless conversant in sixteen languages. Sadly, most of the individuals whom researchers think are worth noting have an impairment that by the deficit it creates tells us something about how language normally works in the brain. But occasionally there are cases in the medical literature so odd that it is difficult to see what can be made of them. That's the case with a condition called Foreign Accent Syndrome.

There have been a handful of people with Foreign Accent Syndrome identified over the last ninety years. These are people who, when they resume speaking after a slight stroke or some other injury to the brain, speak with a foreign accent! And these are not just English speakers who sound as though they are just learning the language as they recover. There were, early in the century, a Frenchman who, after a stroke, spoke with an

Alsatian accent, and a Czech butcher who began to speak with a Polish accent. A thirty-year-old Norwegian woman suffered a head injury during an air raid in 1941, and picked up a German accent. She reported—apparently with some bitterness—that shopkeepers would refuse to serve her. There have been Chinese, New England and even English accents in native Spanish speakers, although the majority of accents seem to be German or Scandinavian. Some of the people affected lose their accent after a while, some don't.

A typical case was reported in 1990 by Dean Tippett, a doctor at the University of Maryland.[70] A thirty-three-year-old man had an attack of slurred speech and unsteadiness, which he first attributed to complications resulting from his diabetes. But it appeared again the following day, and when he went to hospital, it was noticed that his right arm had lost some feeling and strength. A brain scan revealed a slight stroke, and after two months of therapy, the only symptom that remained was weakness in his right arm. But for the first month after the stroke, this man, an American, spoke with what the doctors called a "Nordic" accent.

Everything else, including reading, writing, comprehension and the ability to talk fluently, was normal. But he had this accent, and the rhythm and tone of his speech had become altered: it was singsong, with misplaced stresses on words, and inappropriate tones, rising at the ends of sentences instead of falling. So he would say, "canoe" with the stress on the first syllable: "CA-noo."

Pronunciations were wrong: "hill" became "heel," "quite" became "quiet," and he would stick an "a" in unusual places, like, "How are you today a?" He even substituted "d" for "th," as in "dat" for "that." Put these all together, and you can see where his speech would have taken on what would seem to be a Scandinavian sound, at least to English speakers. Apparently this patient enjoyed having an accent, and just as well, because he didn't seem to have any control over it.

What's going on here? Are these people revisiting an earlier life in a foreign country or what? Obviously linguists don't put *that* forward as an explanation for Foreign Accent Syndrome. In fact, it seems clear that these people are not really speaking with a true accent, but rather that these temporary changes in speech are misidentified by listeners as a foreign accent, because there are one or two features that remind us of accented English. People with true foreign accents hear the difference right away. The human brain has a great capacity for taking in unusual information and making some sort of sense of it, and it's probably true that this altered speech is closest to English as spoken with a foreign accent, so that's how we perceive it. We are very acute at hearing accented speech—one study showed that as little as twenty-thousandths of a second of French-accented English is all we need to hear to know there's an accent there.

One of those features that would make this kind of speech sound to us like Nordic or German accented English would be changes in vowel sounds ("hill" to "heel"). There are probably others too: this sort of speech contains grammatical errors and some deletions of syllables, mistakes that are typical of someone whose first language is not English, and this would tend to confirm any perception that there is an accent present, especially since the rhythm and tone changes make the speech more singsong, again something that isn't typical of a native English speaker.

The damage to the brain that causes Foreign Accent Syndrome is usually in the left hemisphere, but there doesn't seem to be any one location that causes it. The odd thing is that it happens to relatively young people—two-thirds of the cases reported have been under forty-five—yet the strokes that usually cause it are very rare in that age group. It might be that Foreign Accent Syndrome is what we hear as the injured brain recovers from a stroke, an ability that has been lost in an older person.

A Guide to the Proper Use of *You Know* in Sports Interviews

People think guys like us in professional sports don't really give, you know, good interviews, and they think we don't know how to communicate, mostly, uh because we say, "you know" and "sort of" and "like" a lot. Well, maybe if the questions were smarter, eh? Then we wouldn't have to fill in with all that stuff. But I'll tell you something: anyone who criticizes people for using "you know" doesn't know what he's talking about. I mean, it works just about anywhere, but you gotta know where to put it. I'm here to tell you that if you're gonna, you know, use "you know" in your interviews, you gotta do it right. So here goes:

The most important thing to remember is that when you say "you know," it sounds like the interviewer's supposed to know what you're talking about. This is perfect, because then you don't have to think of anything new to say. Lemme give you an example: between periods, the interviewer says to you,

"What are you gonna do in the next period?"

Whatta dumb question, eh? So you say:

"Well, you know (*of course* he knows), we're just gonna come out and give it a hundred and ten, you know, percent, and play hard, and see, you know, what happens."

Perfect. He'll think twice about asking you that question again. Or will he? That's using "you know" to suggest that the guy interviewing you should already know what you're talking about, and for that purpose you can just about stick it in anywhere.

It's also kinda useful when you can't think of anything to say. Like let's say some sports writer says:

"So do you think you have a chance of going all the way this year?"

Well, what are you going to say to that? I mean, if you're playing with an eighteenth-place team that has traded away its first-round draft choices until 2013, you know, whaddya say? You say:

"Uh, well, you know, we're going to go out this year and play hard right from opening day, you know and you know we'll unnhh ... you know, just give a hundred and ten, you know, percent and play good defensive, you know, ball, and score some points."

Great! That's a perfect illustration of "you know" both as a filler and as a device to suggest that the dummy who asked you the question already knows the answer. It also keeps them on their toes when you say "you know" because it sounds like you want a reaction from them. It's like you're saying, "Do you know that?" Those interviewers don't like that, because they're already rehearsing the next question in their head. So when you slip in "you know" they panic, and start nodding their heads and blinking. This is why "you know" is better than "sort of," "like," "kind of" or "I mean" (although I like them all), because none of them sound like, you know, you're asking the interviewer a question.

"You know" is also great in case you forget what you were saying, because you can just stick it in and start on something completely different, and hardly anybody will notice:

"Here's the replay of that last touchdown, can

you tell us how it happened?"

"Well, you know, they'd been overplaying us on the left side all day, so, ahhh, *you know*, we gotta go out and give it a hundred and ten you know percent in the next half. You know, just take it as it comes."

Terrific. And I just gotta tell you one more thing: there're people out there who actually make money figuring this stuff out, and even *they* can't agree on how to use "you know." I mean, one woman studies it in the 1970s and says that women use "you know" a lot more than men—like five times as much—and she's says it's because when guys stop listening to them, they start to get desperate, and stick "you knows" in all over the place just to get their attention! You know she talks about a conversation between a guy and some woman, and the guy only opens his mouth about six times, and, like, she gets desperate and comes out with "you know" *sixteen* times in five minutes. She could be on Hockey Night in Canada! But then some other researcher turns around—another woman—and does a study and says, unh huh, that's not the way it is. Men say "you know" as much as women do (we always knew that, eh?), but get this, that women use it to emphasize that they're sure they're right, but the men in this study used "you know" because they weren't exactly sure about what they were saying. I dunno, maybe it's because these were New Zealand guys.[71] But so what eh? I figure the best thing, you know, is just to keep using "you know" as much as you can, you know, and uh, let those university types figure out what's going on. You know?

The Aquatic Ape and Her Voice-Box

It isn't just our brains that are specialized for talk: we have a space above the voice-box, or larynx, that allows for the production of some of the most important speech sounds. This space was created during the evolution of modern humans when the larynx dropped lower in the throat, presumably at the same time the skull was changing position atop the spinal column to make a right angle between head and spine. The argument has been made again and again that the chimpanzees and the other great apes are not able to articulate the full human range of speech sounds because their larynx sits high in the throat, and there just isn't room for this sound chamber above it to make those sounds. As I described in Chapter Thirteen, this same argument has been applied to the Neanderthal people, the implication being that because their speech abilities were restricted, they came out second-best in the competition with physically modern people.

It's obviously a good thing for the way we produce speech that this downward migration of the larynx happened, but it's a little puzzling why it happened, because it brings with it some disadvantages too, the main one being that we, alone among the primates, run the risk of getting food in our airway because it passes directly over the opening to the larynx on its way down the food tube to the stomach. It is apparently not uncommon for medical students dissecting a cadaver to find a piece of steak blocking the larynx. Before the larynx was situated so low, food couldn't have blocked the airway. Charles Darwin noticed that this was not a perfect place for the larynx, and commented that there must have been a powerful reason for the larynx to move down to this new and riskier position. Obviously because it made better speech possible, right? That would be fine as long as you could be confident that speech and the movement of the larynx were happening at the same time, so that the advantages of one would offset the disadvantages of the other, but it's not at all clear that's how it happened.

There are arguments that suggest that the changes in the position of the larynx and the tongue were happening at the same time as the brain was getting bigger, more powerful and better at communication, and that in fact these reinforced each other: clearer and more varied sounds could provide better information to others, especially if the brain wiring both to perceive and to produce complicated sounds was developing at the same time. But not everyone buys this explanation: some anatomists are much more inclined to point to the radical re-orientation of our bodies when we began to stand on two legs as the cause of the descent of the larynx. To compensate for upright posture, the human skull had to be repositioned so that it sits on top of the spinal column and looks out, as opposed to being in line with the spine like a dog or cat. This severely squeezed the bottom of the skull, with the result that the tongue had to retreat partway down the throat; according to this scenario, because the tongue then threatened to block the opening to the larynx, there was nothing else for the larynx to do but retreat as well. This anatomical explanation depends not at all on the ability to speak. So, was it speech or was it standing up that caused our larynx to drop down—or was it something else again?

Elaine Morgan is author of *The Aquatic Ape*, a book first published in 1980 that argues that at one point in our evolutionary past we lived in the water—not a view shared by many scientists who specialize in human evolution. The idea was first put forward by Sir Alistair Hardy in 1929 (and again independently by a German, Max Westenhofer, in 1942), and it has going for it what many renegade theories have: a number of details that, at least at first glance, make sense. We have a layer of fat under the skin—so do aquatic mammals. We have hairless skin, a streamlined shape, and every once in a while a child will be born with webs of skin between the fingers or toes. Even the human appetite for drinking water and profuse sweat production have been argued to be features that would have been distinctly disadvantageous on the hot African savannah, where our ancestors are thought by most to have lived, but harmless in an environment where water was available in unlimited quantities. All of these characteristics have been interpreted by Elaine Morgan (and the handful of specialists who agree with her) to mean that we spent considerable time in our ancient past wading and swimming in near-shore waters.

Which brings us to the larynx. Elaine Morgan dismisses the anatomical argument for the descent of the larynx (why couldn't the tongue just have shrunk instead of threatening to block the larynx, she wonders?) and instead suggests that it makes much more sense that the larynx dropped to accommodate the unique breathing requirements of living in the water.[72] When the larynx is high in the throat, it connects directly with the nose, leaving the mouth to connect with the food tube (allowing babies to suckle and breathe simultaneously). As soon as the larynx drops, it's then possible to breathe through the mouth, and that makes it possible to gulp huge lungfuls of air if you're going to dive, or as soon as you've come back to the surface of the water *after* diving. So a lowered larynx is a good adaptation for the heavy breathing needed for spending long periods of time underwater.

A second important step in an aquatic life would have been the development of very fine control over the mouth and throat, to control breathing for swimming and diving. These events would have been happening long before our ancestors were capable of speech, but Elaine Morgan thinks they set the stage for it. Once fine control over mouth-breathing was in place, that ability could be turned to controlling the flow of air in and out of the lungs during speech. And remember, that control is *very* fine: different speech sounds are often differentiated by a delay of a few thousandths of a second in the puff of air that sets the vocal cords buzzing. Once back on land, the rapid inhaling and slow exhaling that served these hominids so well in the water could then be turned to speech.

It may sound crazy to you—it definitely sounds crazy to many scientists—but remember this: if you go on the evidence, it's no worse than any other theory for the descent of the larynx. And it's more fun.

Which Hand Do *You* Use for the Telephone?

It's been known since the 1860s that the primary language centres are on the left side of the brain, at least in the vast majority of people. But it was only in the 1960s and 1970s that it became clear that there's a difference between ears as well.

The evidence comes from a variety of sources: tests done in the early sixties in Britain to evaluate new telephone technologies revealed that volunteers who held the telephone to the right ear heard what was coming over the line as if it were three decibels higher than if they used their left ear. On a telephone line, that's a big difference. Then psychologists like Doreen Kimura at the University of Western Ontario began to do experiments on ear advantage in the lab. Volunteers would be asked to put on headphones, and then a different sound would be fed to each ear—usually something like the two syllables **ba** and **da**. When you hear **ba** in one ear, and **da** in the other, you don't hear a mixture, or one superimposed on the other. You hear one only, and it's almost always the one that is presented to your right ear. In some other experiments the sounds presented to the right ear were remembered better than those which went to the left. In general the right ear has a bigger advantage in hearing isolated speech sounds than other kinds of sounds, even when the speech is played backwards. The left ear, by contrast, has an advantage with non-speech sounds, like dog barks, train whistles and music.

To understand why one ear should have an advantage over the other when it comes to speech, you have to trace the wiring of the ears to the brain. Each ear sends signals to both hemispheres of the brain, but the connection to the *opposite* hemisphere is stronger. Sounds coming in the left ear are sent primarily to the brain's right hemisphere but also, although more weakly, to the left hemisphere. Doreen Kimura also added the idea that when sounds were coming in via both ears simultaneously, the weaker, same-side pathway would be suppressed, exaggerating the difference that was already there. This would mean that the sound **ba** presented to the left ear would find its way to the right hemisphere, where there are no major speech centres. At the same time, **da** would enter the right ear and go directly to the speech hemisphere on the left, meaning that **da** is what we would hear. Now it is possible that the information about such a sound could get to the left hemisphere of the brain from the left ear, by a circuitous route to the right hemisphere first, then back across the major connecting cable in the brain, the corpus callosum. But that takes time, and because the two sounds were presented simultaneously, the perception of one has already taken place.

All of this brings us back to one of the original observations from the 1960s: that people using the telephone in Britain found that the same conversation seemed much louder when they held the receiver to their right ear rather than their left. It's not exactly the same kind of evidence as the listening tests, but it supports the idea of a right-ear advantage. But does that mean that most people hold the telephone in the right hand, to gain the advantage of sending the speech they're listening to directly to their speech hemisphere? Apparently not: in a study in 1981 of 337 adults, sixty-three percent of those surveyed preferred holding the phone in their left hand. But there are of course extenuating circumstances: many of these people explained that they wanted to keep the right hand free for dialling, writing or smoking, making it doubtful that the experiment said anything directly about ear preference. This set the stage for another and more intriguing telephone experiment.

In 1987 Jeanette Seeman and Walter Surwillo published the results of a study which looked at the ear preference of airline reservations agents who used "hands-free" headsets for their telephone conversations.[73] There were 294 of them, agents for Republic Airlines in California. Again, more than half—fifty-nine percent—plugged the phone into the left ear. And the agents who preferred the left ear were the more experienced. When you consider that these people are on the phone all day, you'd think that a right-ear advantage for speech should show up, but it clearly didn't. The experimenters asked the 294 agents why they used the ear they did: 106 claimed they had no particular reason to favour one ear or the other, and only 30 said they did it because they could hear better. There were other reasons cited, such as the phone cord getting in the way, but Seeman and Surwillo pointed out that the phone hook-up could easily have been switched to the other side.

The findings are puzzling: the authors suggest that the nature of airline agents' work might explain the results. They spend most of their time figuring out the best combination of flights to take the passenger from A to B to C and back to A again. This reasoning requires skill in spatial relationships, something that is generally believed to be one of the strengths of the right hemisphere. But the tentative nature of this suggestion in their paper hints that even Seeman and Surwillo were a little puzzled by the result. Whichever ear you've chosen to use, the habit is very hard to break (try holding the phone in the "wrong" hand—you'll usually notice in a few moments that, unbeknownst to you, you've switched back). Could it be that the airline agents found the habit of years of left-ear listening (adopted in the first place to leave the right hand free) just too hard to break? But if that were true, why were the inexperienced agents, those you'd expect to be still closely tied to former habits, more likely to be using the right ear? As far as I know, this mystery has never been cleared up.

Conclusion

<<< The Tower of Babel

"And the whole earth was of one language, and of one speech. And it came to pass, as they journeyed from the east, they found a plain in the land of Shinar; and they dwelt there. And they said to one another, Go to, let us make brick, and burn them thoroughly ... let us build us a city and a tower, whose top may reach unto heaven; and let us make a name, lest we be scattered abroad upon the face of the whole earth. And the Lord came down to see the city and the tower, which the children of men builded. And the Lord said, Behold, the people is one, and they have all one language; and this they begin to do ... let us go down, and there confound their language, that they may not understand one another's speech. So the Lord scattered them abroad from thence upon the face of all the earth: and they left off to build the city. Therefore is the name of it called Babel; because the Lord did there confound the language of all the earth ..."

This is the passage from Chapter Eleven of Genesis that describes the destruction of the Tower of Babel, the incident in which mere mortals, having dared to challenge the Lord, were scattered all over the earth, their single language confused into many mutually incomprehensible tongues. Even though the Tower is never mentioned again in the Bible, it was a powerful image.[74] In the sixteen and seventeen hundreds some of the greatest artists in Europe put their concept of the Tower on canvas: the darkest and most magnificent were two portraits by Pieter Brueghel in the 1570s. His were massive, foreboding buildings swarming with men, and rising, even though incomplete, higher than the clouds. They are reminiscent of the Colosseum in Rome: thousands of high arched doorways opening onto a ramp spiralling from bottom to top. Towers as arrogant, dark and dangerous as these would attract the attention of any deity.

There was a Tower of Babel, but unfortunately we will probably never know exactly what it looked like. It was built in the city of Babylon, southwest of modern Baghdad, some time before the seventh century BC. It was a ziggurat, a tower shaped like an eight-layer wedding cake. Ziggurats were probably places of worship, the ancient versions of cathedrals. The most reliable description of the Tower of Babel comes from Herodotus, the traveller and historian who visited Babylon in 460 BC. He wrote:

"In the midst of the temple a solid tower was constructed, one stadium in length and one stadium in width. Upon this tower stood another, and again upon this another, and so on, making eight towers in all, one upon another. All eight towers can be climbed by means of a spiral staircase which runs round the outside. About halfway up there are seats where those who make the ascent can sit and rest. In the topmost tower there is a great temple, and in the temple is a great bed richly appointed, and beside it a golden table ..."

It's always risky to depend on eyewitness accounts, let alone from twenty-four centuries ago, but Herodotus's account has been given some credibility by a stone tablet from 229 BC. The tablet lists the length, breadth and height of each of seven storeys of the ziggurat of Babylon. They are of course quoted in measurements alien to us (suklum-cubits) but they translate to a tower that was nearly two hundred and ninety-five feet square at the bottom, and two hundred and ninety-five feet high: the length, width and height of a football field. It's possible, given the uncertainties of translation, that a temple stood on top of the seventh storey. That would make the total number of layers square with Herodotus's account.

But where is it now? Centuries of explorers searched the plains of what had been Mesopotamia (now Iraq) looking for the Tower of Babel, with the first serious excavations beginning in the middle of the nineteenth century. It wasn't until 1899 that the German archaeologist R. Koldewey found the Tower—or rather, he located the pile of bricks that is all that is left of it. It wasn't just that the Tower was in ruins—it was already known that Xerxes had given the orders for its demolition shortly before Herodotus is supposed to have seen it—the locals had discovered that the Tower's bricks made excellent building materials, and whole towns in the area were constructed mostly of bricks from the Tower of Babel. Nonetheless, Koldewey was able to measure what had been the outline of the base of the tower, and he also found the remains of three staircases. Each wall was 49 feet (16 metres) of an inner filling of sun-dried bricks coated on the outside with baked bricks. But the striking finding was that each wall was 298 feet long, almost exactly the 295 feet recorded in the stone tablet.

Koldewey estimated that the staircases must have risen a hundred feet or more, but that was all the information he could extract from the rubble. No sign of Herodotus's spiral staircase or walk-way—none of the blue enamelled bricks which had reputedly covered the penthouse temple around the time of Nebuchadnezzar II. The Tower of Babel is now just an enormous hole filled with water that seeps in from the nearby Euphrates River.

The ostentatious, militaristic and enormously successful Babylonians were convenient villains for the writers of Genesis, so it's not surprising that blame for the permanent loss of a universal earthly language would be laid at their feet, the people who dared to erect a pagan tower into the heavens. But while the framework of the story is propaganda, the desire to understand the origins and proliferation of languages is the motif.

The same Herodotus who described the Tower of Babel also relates the story of an Egyptian pharaoh, Psammeticus, who, in an attempt to find out which nation was the first on earth, ordered two children to be taken away from their parents and put in the care of a mute shepherd, who was to raise them without any contact with other people. Naturally he was disappointed to find out that the first word they spoke was "bekos," meaning bread in Phrygian (the language spoken by Homer's Trojans), not Egyptian. It's been suggested that the "bekos" could have just been an imitation of the bleating of sheep that must have surrounded these children, so Psammeticus shouldn't have been so upset.

This was only one of several attempts by rulers to establish what language children in isolation would speak. Frederick II of Sicily in the early 1200s, James IV of Scotland in 1493, and Akbar the Great in India in the late 1500s all isolated newborn children or sequestered them with mute adults, and while there were some reports of speech (the two children isolated by James IV were supposed to have spoken "guid" Hebrew), sadly but predictably most of the children died during the experiment. Those sent away by Akbar the Great had dumb nurses with them, and so had no trouble surviving. They learned language too—the nurses taught them how to communicate with signs and gestures. But they didn't talk.

We read these tales told by Herodotus and we think they represent a kind of thinking that is so primitive, so unlike the way we would try to answer those same questions today. But are we really much further ahead? We're still searching for the mother tongue, that language those tower builders were speaking. And you can lump all the fossil skulls, stone tools, talking chimps and reconstructed ancient languages you can find together, and you still won't have an answer. And if you choose to read the story of the Tower of Babel as an account of a single language that, through some sort of dramatic social upheaval, fragmented and spread around the world, you've got the scenario of an African birthplace for the mother tongue and subsequent vast migrations of *Homo sapiens* out of that continent. Just substitute tool-makers for tower builders and you've got it.

And what about poor naïve Psammeticus, and his intellectual descendants? We wouldn't isolate children, nor would we expect that children so deprived would speak any language, let alone the first one. But our fascination with the occasional child who suffers that fate inadvertently—Victor, Genie—speaks volumes. We know Psammeticus was wrong, but we're not sure what's right.

Languages haven't really changed much since Herodotus wrote—they certainly aren't getting any more complicated or sophisticated, they're not evolving to some higher state, they're just there. The extinct ones are just as good as those spoken today. And it turns out that the questions we want answered about language haven't changed much either. As the pilot with the disabled compass said, "Ladies and Gentlemen, the bad news is that we have no idea where we are—the good news is that we're making excellent time."

<<<   # Notes

1. S. Duncan and D. Fiske, "Dynamic Patterning in Conversation," *American Scientist* 67 (Jan.–Feb. 1979): 90–98.
2. G. Jefferson, "A Case of Precision Timing in Conversation: Overlapped Tag-positioned Address Terms in Closing Sequences," *Semiotica* IX (1973): 47–96.
3. A. Cutler and M. Pearson, "On the Analysis of Prosodic Turn-taking Cues," in *Intonation in Discourse*, ed. C. John-Lewis (London: Croom Helm, 1985).
4. G. Beattie, *Talk: an Analysis of Speech and Non-Verbal Behaviour in Conversation* (Milton Keynes: Open University Press, 1983).
5. P. Fishman, "Interaction: The Work Women Do," in *Language, Gender and Society*, eds. N. Henley, C. Kamara and B. Thorne (Rowley, Mass.: Newbury House, 1983) 89–101.
6. C. West and D. Zimmerman, "Small Insults: A Study of Interruptions in Cross-sex Conversa-

tions Between Unacquainted Persons," in *Language, Gender and Society*, 102–117.

7. A. Cutler and D. Scott, "Speaker Sex and Perceived Apportionment of Talk," *Applied Psycholinguistics* 11 (1990): 253–272.

8. G. Beattie, Talk: *An Analysis of Speech and Non-Verbal Behaviour in Conversation* (Milton Keynes: Open University Press, 1983).

9. P. Broca, cited in M. Critchley, *Aphasiology and Other Aspects of Language* (London: Edwin Arnold, 1970).

10. D. Allport and E. Funnell, "Components of the Mental Lexicon," *Philosophical Transactions of the Royal Society of London* B295 (1981): 397–410.

11. H. Gardner, *The Shattered Mind* (New York: Random House, 1974).

12. Ibid.

13. A. Kreindler, et al., "A Linguistic Analysis of One Case of Jargon Aphasia." *Revue Roumaine de Neurologie*, 8 (1971): 209-228.

14. J.W. Brown, *Aphasia, Apraxia and Agnosia*, (Springfield, Ill.: Charles C. Thomas, 1972).

15. H. Neville, in *Brain Maturation and Cognitive Development: Comparative and Cross-Cultural Perspectives*, eds. K.R. Gibson and A.C. Petersen (Hawthorne, N.Y.: Aldine de Gruyter Press, 1991), 355–380.

16. E. Ross, "The Divided Self," *The Sciences* (February 1982), 8–12.

17. J. Hart, R. Berndt and A. Caramazza, "Category-specific Naming Deficit Following

Cerebral Infarction," *NATURE* 316 (1985): 439–440.

18. M. Paradis, "Bilingual and Polyglot Aphasia," in *Handbook of Neuropsychology*, vol. 2, eds. H. Goodglass and A.R. Damasio (Amsterdam: Elsevier, 1989), 117–140.

19. W. Penfield and L. Roberts, *Speech and Brain Mechanisms* (Princeton: Princeton University Press, 1959).

20. G. Ojemann, "Cortical Organization of Language," *The Journal of Neuroscience* 11 (August 1991): 2281–2287.

21. A. Damasio, "Category-related Recognition Defects as a Clue to the Neural Substrates of Knowledge," *Trends in Neurosciences* 13, no. 3 (1990): 95–98.

22. A. Hill, "A theory of Speech Errors," in *Speech Errors as Linguistic Evidence*, ed. V. Fromkin (The Hague: Mouton, 1973).

23. M. Motley, "Slips of the Tongue," *Scientific American* (September 1985): 116–127.

24. O. Koenig, C. Wetzel and A. Caramazza, "Evidence for Different Types of Lexical Representations in the Cerebral Hemispheres," *Cognitive Neuropsychology* 9, no. 1 (1992): 33–45.

25. R. Brown and D. McNeill, "The 'Tip of the Tongue' Phenomenon," *Journal of Verbal Learning and Behavior* 5 (1966): 325–337.

26. C. Renfrew, *Archaeology and Language* (London: Penguin Books, 1987) and J. Mallory, *In Search of the Indo-Europeans* (London:

Thames and Hudson, 1989).

27. R. Sokal, N. Oden and C. Wilson, "Genetic Evidence for the Spread of Agriculture in Europe by Demic Diffusion," *NATURE* 351 (1991): 143–145.

28. D. Anthony, D. Telegin and D. Brown, "The Origin of Horseback Riding," *Scientific American* (December 1991): 94–100.

29. R. Wright, "Quest for the Mother Tongue," *The Atlantic Monthly* (April 1991): 39–68.

30. J. Diamond, "The Talk of the Americas," *NATURE* 344 (1990): 589–590.

31. B. Bower, "America's Talk: The Great Divide," *Science News* (June 9, 1990): 360–362.

32. M. Krauss, "The World's Languages in Crisis," address to the Linguistic Society of America, January 3, 1991, Chicago.

33. V. Shevoroshkin, "The Mother Tongue," *The Sciences* (May–June 1990), 20–27.

34. L. Cavalli-Sforza et al., "Reconstruction of Human Evolution: Bringing Together Genetic, Archaeological and Linguistic Data," *Proceedings of the National Academy of Science* 85 (1988): 6002–6006.

35. M. Gopnik, "Linguistic Properties of Genetic Language Impairment," address to the American Association for the Advancement of Science, February 10, 1992, Chicago.

36. E. Plante, "MRI Findings in the Parents and Siblings of Specifically Language-impaired Boys," *Brain and Language* 41 (1991): 67–80.

37. S. Pinker, "Rules of Language," *Science* 253

(1991): 530–535.

38. N. Toth, "The First Technology," *Scientific American* (April 1987): 112–121.

39. D. Kimura, "Neuromotor Mechanisms in the Evolution of Human Communication," in *Neurobiology of Social Communication in Primates*, eds. H. Steklis and M. Raleigh (New York: Academic Press, 1979).

40. P. Greenfield, "Language, Tools and Brain: The Ontogeny and Phylogeny of Hierarchically Organized Sequential Behavior," *Behavioral and Brain Sciences* 14 (1991): 531–595.

41. D. Premack, "'Gavagai!' or the Future History of the Animal Language Controversy," *Cognition* 19 (1985): 207–296.

42. P. Lieberman, *The Biology and Evolution of Language* (Cambridge, Mass.: Harvard University Press, 1984).

43. B. Arensburg et al., "A Middle Paleolithic Human Hyoid Bone," *NATURE* 338 (1989): 758–760.

44. J. Yamada, "The Independence of Language: Evidence from a Retarded Hyperlinguistic Individual," in *Language, Speech and Mind*, eds. L.M. Hyman and C.N. Li (New York: Routledge, 1988).

45. N. Smith and I. Tsimpli, "Linguistic Modularity? A Case Study of a 'Savant' Linguist," *Lingua* 84 (1991): 315–351.

46. P. Eimas, "The Perception of Speech in Early Infancy," *Scientific American* (January 1985): 46–52.

47. M. Barrett, "Scripts, Prototypes and the Early Acquisition of Word Meaning," *Working Papers of the London Psycholinguistic Research Group* 5 (1983): 17–26.

48. M. Bowerman, "The Structure and Origin of Semantic Categories in the Language Learning Child," in *Symbol as Sense: New Approaches to the Analysis of Meaning*, eds. D. Foster and S. Brandes (New York: Academic Press, 1980).

49. L. Vygotsky, *Thought and Language* (Cambridge, Mass.: MIT Press, 1962).

50. P. Fletcher, "Verb Form Development: Lexis or Grammar?" in *Proceedings of the Second International Congress for the Study of Child Language*, vol. 2, eds. C.I. Phew and C.E. Johnson (Lanham, Maryland: University Press of America, 1983).

51. B. Blank et al., "Language Without Communication: A Case Study," *Journal of Child Language* 6 (1979): 329–352.

52. M. Braine, "The Acquisition of Language in Infant and Child," in *The Learning of Language*, ed. C.E. Reed (New York: Appleton-Century-Crofts, 1971).

53. J. Bruner, "Learning the Mother Tongue," *Human Nature* (September 1978): 42–49.

54. E. Newport, H. Gleitman and L. Gleitman, "Mother I'd Rather Do It Myself: Some Effects and Noneffects of Maternal Speech Style," in *Talking to Children: Language Input and Acquisition*, ed. C.E. Snow and C.A. Ferguson (Cambridge, Mass.: Cambridge University

Press, 1977).

55. H. Lane, *The Wild Boy of Aveyron* (Cambridge, Mass.: Harvard University Press, 1976) and R. Shattuck, *The Forbidden Experiment: The Story of the Wild Boy of Aveyron* (New York: Farrar, Straus and Giroux, 1980).

56. S. Curtiss, *Genie: A Psycholinguistic Study of a Modern-Day Wild Child* (New York: Academic Press, 1977).

57. C. Warden and L. Warner, "The Sensory Capacities and Intelligence of Dogs, with a Report on the Ability of the Noted Dog 'Fellow' to Respond to Verbal Stimuli," *The Quarterly Review of Biology* III (March 1928): 1–28.

58. H. Terrace et al., "Can an Ape Create a Sentence?" *Science* 206 (1979): 891–902.

59. P. Lieberman, *The Biology and Evolution of Language* (Cambridge, Mass.: Harvard University Press, 1984), 241.

60. E. Sue Savage-Rumbaugh, "Pan to Man: The Language Link," address to the American Association for the Advancement of Science, February 8, 1992, Chicago.

61. M. Seidenberg and L. Petitto, "Communication, Symbolic Communication and Language," *Journal of Experimental Psychology: General* 116 (1987): 279–287.

62. D. Bickerton, *Language and Species* (Chicago: University of Chicago Press, 1990).

63. R. Hall, "Pidgin Languages," *Scientific American* (February 1959): 124–134.

64. T. Posey and M. Losch, "Auditory Hallucinations of Hearing Voices in 375 Normal Subjects," *Imagination, Cognition and Personality* 2 (1983): 99–113.

65. R. Korba, "The Rate of Inner Speech," *Perceptual and Motor Skills* 71 (1990): 1043–1052.

66. J. Cacioppo and R. Petty, "Electromyograms as Measures of Extent and Affectivity of Information Processing," *American Psychologist* 36 (1981): 441–456.

67. P. Green and M. Preston, "Reinforcement of Vocal Correlates of Auditory Hallucinations by Auditory Feedback: A Case Study," *British Journal of Psychiatry* 139 (1981): 204–208.

68. F. Henker, "Joan of Arc and DSM III," *Southern Medical Journal* 77 (1984): 1488–1490.

69. H.N. Malony and A.A. Lovekin, *Glossolalia: Behavioral Science Perspectives on Speaking in Tongues* (New York: Oxford University Press, 1985) and W. Samarin, *Tongues of Men and Angels: The Religious Language of Pentecostalism* (New York: Macmillan, 1972).

70. D. Tippett and K. Yeakle, "Foreign Accent Syndrome Following a Left Internal Capsule Infarct," presented to the American Neurological Association, October 1990, Atlanta.

71. J. Holmes, "Functions of *You Know* in Women's and Men's Speech," *Language in Society* 15 (1986): 1–22.

72. E. Morgan, "Why a New Theory is Needed," in *The Aquatic Ape: Fact or Fiction*, eds. M.

Roede et al. (London: Souvenir Press, 1991).

73. J. Seeman and W. Surwillo, "Ear Preference in Telephone Listening," *Perceptual and Motor Skills* 65 (1987): 803–809.

74. A. Parrot, *The Tower of Babel* (London: SCM Press, 1955).

Selected Reading

There are very few books for general readers that cover the breadth of language research, but there are several that provide good accounts of specific research areas.

Aitchison, Jean. *Words in the Mind: An Introduction to the Mental Lexicon.* Oxford: Basil Blackwell, 1987. Dr Aitchison writes about where words might be stored in the brain, how we retrieve them and what can go wrong. She is one of the few in this field who writes with a sense of humour.

Auel, Jean M. *The Clan of The Cave Bear.* New York: Crown Publishers, Inc., 1980. Along with this, you should read William Golding's *The Inheritors* and palaeontologist Björn Kurtén's *Dance of the Tiger.* Together, the three are a perfect guide to the change in ideas about the Neanderthals from the fifties to the eighties.

Beattie, Geoffrey. *Talk: An Analysis of Speech and Non-Verbal Behaviour in Communication.* London: Open University Press, 1983. This has good accounts of Beattie's Margaret Thatcher research and other experiments, but it may be difficult to find in North America.

Crystal, David, ed. *The Cambridge Encyclopaedia of Language*. Cambridge: Cambridge University Press, 1987. This is a true encyclopaedia: you don't want to read it through, but it's great for short accounts of specific topics.

Curtiss, Susan. *Genie: A Psycholinguistic Study of a Modern-Day Wild Child*. New York: Academic Press, 1977. This is in many places a very technical book, but it's the definitive report of Curtiss's work with Genie.

Fry, Dennis. *Homo Loquens*. Cambridge: Cambridge University Press, 1977. Fry writes very clearly and non-technically about the production and perception of speech, but again this may be a difficult book to find.

Golding, William. *The Inheritors*. London: Faber and Faber, 1955.

Jaynes, Julian. *The Origins of Consciousness in the Breakdown of the Bicameral Mind*. Boston: Houghton Mifflin, 1976. This book has been around for a while now, but the idea that at one time we got through life by listening to auditory hallucinations is still fascinating enough that, as a psychologist told me a long time ago, "Who cares if it isn't right?"

Kurtén, Björn. *Dance of the Tiger*. New York: Pantheon Books, 1980.

Lane, Harlan. *The Wild Boy of Aveyron*. Cambridge Mass.: Harvard University Press, 1976.

This brings together most of the information that's available about Dr Itard's attempts to teach the wild boy to speak.

Miller, George A. *The Science of Words*. New York: Scientific American Library, 1991. In the tradition of *Scientific American* magazine, this is on the technical side, and also has a fairly narrow focus on the author's interests, but it contains good information and illustrations.

Renfrew, Colin. *Archaeology and Language: The Puzzle of Indo-European Origins*. London: Penguin Books, 1987. There might be more here than you'd ever want to know about Indo-Europeans, but it's the most entertaining book about them.

Samarin, William. *Tongues of Men and Angels: The Religious Language of Pentecostalism*. New York: Macmillan, 1972. There have been more recent books about speaking in tongues, but none really adds a great deal to what Samarin found. He stripped away much of the mysticism and ignorance from the subject.

Stevenson, Victor, ed. *Words: The Evolution of Western Languages*. London: Methuen, 1983. This is the place to start if you're interested in, but not familiar with, the relationships between today's languages.

Tannen, Deborah. *You Just Don't Understand: Women and Men in Conversation*. New York: William Morrow and Company, 1990. This is the best-seller that examines conversations from the point of view that men and women belong to two different cultures.